PORTFOLIO
ARTHASHASTRA

THOMAS R. TRAUTMANN is the author of *Kautilya and the Arthashastra* (1971) and other books on ancient India, including *Aryans and British India* (1997), *The Aryan Debate* (2005), *Languages and Nations: The Dravidian Proof in Colonial Madras* (2006) and *India: Brief History of a Civilization* (2010). He is professor emeritus of history and anthropology at the University of Michigan.

GURCHARAN DAS is a world-renowned author, commentator and public intellectual. His bestselling books include *India Unbound, The Difficulty of Being Good* and *India Grows at Night*. His other literary works consist of a novel, *A Fine Family*, a book of essays, *The Elephant Paradigm*, and an anthology, *Three Plays*. A graduate of Harvard University, Das was CEO of Procter & Gamble, India, before he took early retirement to become a full-time writer. He lives in Delhi.

THE STORY OF INDIAN BUSINESS
Series Editor: Gurcharan Das

THE STORY OF INDIAN BUSINESS

ARTHASHASTRA

The Science of Wealth

THOMAS R. TRAUTMANN

Introduction by
Gurcharan Das

PORTFOLIO
PENGUIN

An imprint of Penguin Random House

PORTFOLIO

USA | Canada | UK | Ireland | Australia
New Zealand | India | South Africa | China | Singapore

Portfolio is part of the Penguin Random House group of companies
whose addresses can be found at global.penguinrandomhouse.com

Published by Penguin Random House India Pvt. Ltd
4th Floor, Capital Tower 1, MG Road,
Gurugram 122 002, Haryana, India

Penguin
Random House
India

First published in Allen Lane by Penguin Books India 2012
Published in Portfolio 2016

ISBN 9780143426189

Typeset in Aldine401 BT by SÜRYA, New Delhi

Printed at Manipal Technologies Limited, India

www.penguin.co.in

MIX
Paper | Supporting
responsible forestry
FSC® C043100

This is a legitimate digitally printed version of the book and therefore might not
have certain extra finishing on the cover.

CONTENTS

CONTENTS

INTRODUCTION

In the happiness of his subjects lies the king's happiness, in their welfare his welfare. He shall not consider as good only that which pleases him but treat as beneficial to him whatever pleases his subjects.

—Arthashastra, I.19.34

The story of Indian business

Since the *Arthashastra* is the world's first manual in political economy, it is appropriate that Tom Trautmann's radiant study of this text is placed first in our multi-volume series. Our story of Indian business, based on a close examination of texts, is about the great business and economic ideas that have shaped commerce on the Indian subcontinent.

In this series, leading contemporary scholars interpret

texts and ideas in a lively, sharp and authoritative manner, for the intelligent reader with no prior background in the field. Each slender volume recounts the romance and adventure of business enterprise in the bazaar or on the high seas along a 5,000-mile coastline. Each author offers an enduring perspective on business and economic enterprise in the past, avoiding the pitfall of simplistically cataloguing a set of lessons for today. The value of the exercise, if we are successful, will be to promote in the reader a longer-term sensibility, which can help understand the material bases for our present human condition and think sensibly about the future. Taken together, the Story of Indian Business series celebrates the ideal captured in the Sanskrit word *artha*, material well-being, which was one of the aims of the classical Indian life.

The books in this series range over a vast territory—beginning two thousand years ago with this volume on the ancient art of wealth and ending with the Bombay Plan, drawn in 1944–45 by eminent industrialists who wrestled with the proper roles of the public and private sectors—recounted for us vividly by Medha Kudaisiya. In-between is a veritable feast. In addition to the *Arthashastra*, four sparkling volumes cover the ancient and the early medieval periods—Gregory Schopen presents the *Business Model of Early Buddhist Monasticism* based on the *Mulasarvastivada-vinya*; Kanakalatha Mukund, drawing from the epics *Silappadikaram* and *Manimekalai*, takes us into the world of the Tamil merchant to the end of the Chola empire; Himanshu Prabha Ray transfers us to the maritime-trading world of the western Indian ocean along the Kanara and Gujarat coasts, using the Sanskrit *Lekhapaddhati* written in Gujarati; and Arshia Sattar recounts the brilliant adventures told in *The Mouse Merchant* and in other tales based on the *Kathasaritsagara* and other sources.

Scott Levi takes off into the early modern period with the saga of Multani traders in caravans through central Asia, rooted in the work of Zia al-Din Barani's *Tarikh-i-Firuz Shahi* and Jean-Baptiste Tavernier. The celebrated Sanjay Subrahmanyam and Muzaffar Alam transport us into the world of sultans, shopkeepers and portfolio capitalists in Mughal India. Ishan Chakrabarti traces the ethically individualistic world of Banarsidas, a Jain merchant in Mughal times, via his diary, *Ardhakathanak*. Tirthankar Roy's elegant volume on the East India Company is our passage to the modern world, where the distinguished Lakshmi Subramaniam recounts the ups and downs in the adventurous lives of three great merchants of Bombay—Tarwady Arjunjee Nathjee, Jamsetjee Jeejeebhoy and Premchand Raychand.

Anuradha Kumar adds to this a narrative on the

building of railways in nineteenth-century India through the eyes of those who built them. Chhaya Goswami dives deep into the Indian Ocean to recount the tale of Kachchhi enterprise in the triangle between Zanzibar, Muscat and Mandvi. Tom Timberg revisits the bold, risk-taking world of the Marwaris and Raman Mahadevan describes Nattukottai Chettiars' search for fortune. Vikramjit Banerjee rounds up the series with competing visions of prosperity among men who fought for India's freedom in the early twentieth century via the works of Gandhi, Vivekenanda, Nehru, Ambedkar and others. The privilege of reading these rich and diverse volumes has left me—one reader—with a sense of wonder at the vivid, dynamic and illustrious role played by trade and economic enterprise in advancing Indian civilization.

Arthashastra, property and the king's share

In this introduction I shall not go over the same ground as Professor Trautmann's graceful and authoritative work but focus instead on a few themes which provide context for his book and will hopefully enrich the experience of reading it. I shall confine myself to three issues: 1) Given that the notion of property is central to a market economy, it is worth asking the question: what was the status of private property and especially land tenure in the society of the *Arthashastra*? 2) What are the principles of leadership which emanate from the *Arthashastra*? Although these were intended as advice to a royal prince, I believe they are applicable to all political and business leaders. 3) Early in his book, Trautmann reminds us that *artha*, material well-being, is one of the three or four classical goals of life and it is subordinate to *dharma*, moral well-being. I shall reflect on the significance of the primacy of dharma over artha.

The polity of the *Arthashastra* is a mixture of private enterprise and state control. What the right mixture ought to be has been the subject of intense debate between the Left and the Right in contemporary politics. No matter where one is situated in the debate, most people believe that a sense of security is not only good in itself but also contributes to prosperity in a free society. Individuals will invest when they feel secure— when they believe that their property will not be taken away arbitrarily. The state is expected to make citizens feel secure, but often it is the principal cause of insecurity, particularly when it does not enforce property rights or when it acquires private land without just cause or adequate compensation. In some societies, the king was believed to own all the land, and this contributed to the insecurity of land tenure. The question is: how secure was property, especially land tenure, in ancient India? Given the scarcity of empirical evidence, one can only speculate on the basis of norms articulated in the dharma texts.

Professor Trautmann offers a sparkling clue from the *Arthashastra* when he introduces the notion of the king's bhaga, share, suggesting that the state was only one among many shareholders, and there was a separation of the individual's from the king's property. This is quite different from societies where the king owned all property. Bhaga suggests a limitation of state power over the property of others, which is reaffirmed in other dharma texts. Normally the king's share was one-sixth, *shad-bhagin*, and this proportion carried into the tax levied by the state on the produce of the land as well as on other economic transactions.

Trautmann rightly calls the concept of bhaga 'entrepreneurial'. For the focus 'is not on ownership of a resource but of a share of what is produced . . . [and] at the heart of the idea of the share [is] a certain sense of mutual interest among co-sharers to promote production, as then all shares will be larger'. He adds, 'it is a language drawn from fathers and sons working on agricultural land or partnership of traders and merchants'. The notion of bhaga has its focal point on possession, not on ownership. Ownership means that one can sell the property; possession does not. Bhaga indicates occupation and use of the property, and to ensure that the householder had a sense of security in possession, the king is told not to interfere in the *Naradasmriti*: 'A householder's house and his field are considered as the two fundamentals of his existence. Therefore let not the king upset either of them.'

How the notion of king's share and by implication the security of individual property arose in ancient India is hard to say. Professor R.P. Kangle, editor of the critical edition of the *Arthashastra*, thinks that 'it may go back to an earlier stage in the development of society when all land was the property of the entire tribe . . . [and] over the generations individual families continued to hold and till the same separate pieces of land, until a vested interest was created, which practically amounted to ownership of the separate pieces of land. Then the rights of alienation came to be recognized.'[1] This may be how land became private property to be bought and sold, although there are few references in the dharma literature to the sale of property. We can be sure about the security of possession but not about ownership.

The *Arthashastra* speaks about four land arrangements: the king's land, lands of private individuals, common land and unoccupied forest land. We have touched upon the first two; the third refers to the existence of common lands around every village for the enjoyment of everyone;[2] the fourth are uninhabited lands, often in the forest. Some of the confusion about the status of private property in ancient India has arisen because the *Arthashastra* and other texts refer to the grants of these lands. The *Arthashastra* says the king may grant his subjects vacant land if they are willing to clear it, till it and pay a tax on it. If they fail to develop the land, it would be taken away and given to others.[3] The ability to grant land gave rise to the mistaken idea that the king was the owner of all the land in ancient India.

Megasthenes, the Greek ambassador to the Mauryan court, was the first to state that Indian kings owned the whole land of the country. But Megasthenes was not a reliable reporter, and some of what he wrote was fantastic nonsense, including an account of gold-digging ants in India that were the size of foxes. A.L. Basham, the respected English scholar, says: 'More than one source speaks of the king as the owner of all the land and water in his kingdom' but he also added that a few texts reject the king's ownership of all the land. The mistake of the those who believed in royal ownership of all land was apparently based on misreading the dharma texts, which speak of the king as pati, 'lord' or swami, 'master' of the whole kingdom. Their error was to believe that pati or swami implies an 'owner', when it means 'protector' of the kingdom.[4]

Other dharma texts and legal commentators argue eloquently that the king does not own the land of the kingdom. Shabaraswami, an authoritative commentator on the *Purva Mimasa*, says, 'The monarch has not property on the earth ... His kingly power is for government of the realm and extirpation of wrongs; and for that purpose he receives taxes from husbandmen and levies fines from offenders. But the right of property is not thereby vested in him.' Later commentators express similar views. Nilakantha, a legal scholar in sixteenth century, specifically mentions private property of other landlords: 'Proprietary right in the whole land with regard to villages, lands, etc., lies in their respective landlords. The King's right is limited to the collection of tax therefrom.' Finally, Madhava, the eminent jurist, also refers to limitations in the king's power over private land. 'King's sovereignty is for correcting the wicked and fostering the good. Hence, the land is not king's wealth ... [It is] the common wealth of all living beings to enjoy the fruit of their labour.'[5]

Ancient India, as it emerges from the normative dharma texts, seems thus to present a world quite different world from that of 'Oriental Despotism', a term that the ancient Greeks used contemptuously to refer to the states of Asia and the Middle East, and particularly their enemy, the Persian Empire, where 'the king owned all and everyone was his slave'. By characterizing Asians in this manner, the Greeks were flattering themselves—they were contrasting their own status as free citizens with Asian slavery. Marx took up the idea of Oriental Despotism, calling it the 'Asiatic mode of production' to explain why 'Asia fell asleep in history'. The Asiatic mode referred in particular to the agrarian empires of ancient Egypt and China, where an absolute ruler farmed out the right to collect tribute from peasants to a hierarchy of petty officials, and where extorting tribute from village communities became the mode of enrichment for the ruling nobility.

When the British came to India they continued with the historical mistake of believing that India too was under 'Oriental Despotism', and this guided their thinking about land tenure. The recent work of historians suggests, however, that property rights to land were generally more secure in India and the major Eurasian agrarian societies—China, Japan, the Ottoman Empire and Europe—than was once believed. It is in the context of this debate that we should note the statement of the *Arthashastra*, an avowedly royalist text, that the king's land is separate from common lands and individual holdings.

How much land an individual should own is a different question, and did not concern the ancients in India or elsewhere. Perhaps, this was because land was plentiful. But with the passing of time and a growth in population, this question began to occupy the minds of men. In seventeenth-century England, John Locke, the political philosopher who is regarded as the father of modern liberalism, offered an elegant answer. He said that private property is derived from human labour. In his *Second Treatise*, Locke stated: 'As much land as a man tills . . . and can use the product of, so much is his property. He by his labour does, as it were, enclose it from the common.' This came to be known as the 'labour theory of value', about which Karl Marx had much to say later. Locke believed, however, that property precedes government and government cannot 'dispose of the estates of the subjects arbitrarily'. Thus, property is a natural right, he believed, and this right is now enshrined in the Constitutions of all modern states. The main justification of this right is based on the ethical development of the individual or the creation of a social environment in which people can prosper as free and responsible agents.

What makes a good leader?

Leadership is crucial in both business and politics, and the *Arthashastra* obliges by offering a fairly detailed account of the qualities of a good leader. Towards the end of chapter one, Trautmann describes the ideal king, or rajarshi, as 'a king who is a rishi or sage'. In reading over the king's rigorous daily routine, what stands out is the high energy expected of the ruler. The night and the day are divided into eight parts by the sundial in a packed schedule, with constant attention to the business of the day. The ruler is expected to sleep for only four and a half hours. The day's routine includes time for study and recreation, and the text does make a major concession—it allows the king to adjust his pace according to his capacity.[6]

A high energy level seems to be consistent with the exhausting pace maintained by successful business and political leaders throughout history. It is also required of senior managers in modern-day corporations today. What is remarkable about the king's demanding pace in the *Arthashastra* is a commitment to 'secular asceticism', a term that Max Weber, the German sociologist, used to characterize Protestant entrepreneurs. The striking feature of the king's ethic of ceaseless work is that it is accompanied by a ceaseless renunciation of the life of luxury that surrounds him. It is not unlike the renunciation commended by Krishna to Arjuna in the discipline of *nishkama karma*, non-attached action, in the Bhagavad Gita. In my long experience in business, I have found many secular ascetics among the entrepreneurs and senior managers I have known. Aditya Birla, Ratan Tata, Azim Premji and Narayana Murthy are a few examples from the contemporary Indian corporate world—the more successful they became, the more they tended to live frugally. I sometimes feel that the world is divided into producers and consumers— high-performing leaders have little time for consumption.

To achieve this ascetic ideal the king is expected to control his senses, says the *Arthashastra*. He is supposed to lead a life of self-control and keep a check over the human passions of lust, anger, greed, pride and arrogance. In particular, he should avoid associating with another's wife; not covet another's property; practise *ahimsa*, non-violence, towards all living things; and avoid the company of harmful persons. He should especially avoid the four vices which lead to a loss of self-control: gambling, drinking, womanizing and hunting. On the positive side, he should cultivate a life of intellect by a disciplined study of different fields of human knowledge; cultivate the company of wise men; be righteous and honest; and finally, he should be resolute and determined, not dilatory and fickle. If he follows this prescription, he will acquire self-discipline, from which will follow self-possession, a vital quality of leadership.

Leadership is about influencing and motivating people and the *Arthashastra* offers a number of ways that are familiar to both corporate and political leaders. A leader can motivate people through fear and punishment (*danda*) or reward and trust (*dana*). Every leader has faced this dilemma: what is the right balance between the 'carrot' and the 'stick'? The *Arthashastra*, ever suspicious of human nature, mostly veers to the latter end and offers rich discussion about *dandaniti*, retributive justice. It is at pains to point out, however, that punishment should be proportionate to the wrongdoing and be perceived as deserved and just by the public—otherwise, the leader will lose the respect of his people.[7] Consistent with its sceptical nature, it suggests other disagreeable strategies for influencing and controlling people by dividing them (*bheda*), or using deceit and illusion (*maya*). Dictators and leaders of totalitarian regimes are familiar with these strategies.

Why does the goal of dharma trump artha?

Professor Trautmann introduces us at the beginning of his book to the classical doctrine of the four aims of life. Many of the ancient texts, including the *Arthashastra*, discuss the proper place of each of these aims. In particular, they raise the question of whether the pursuit of artha or profit should be governed by dharma or righteousness. I shall briefly examine the significance of the priority given to the ethical dimension in market transactions.

Dharma is a frustrating and untranslatable word. Duty, goodness, justice, law and religion all have something to do with it, but they fall short. I think of it chiefly as a concern for doing the right thing, both in our private and our public lives. Towards the end of chapter five, Trautman discusses dharma in the context of law, in particular, commercial law (*vyavahara*). Disputes are natural in economic transactions and private commercial contracts, and need to be resolved. The *Arthashastra* suggests a panel of three judges called *dharmasthas*, 'upholders of dharma', to resolve disputes. Trautmann wisely reminds us about the crucial role of law and justice in a market economy, something that economists and business people sometimes forget. He says, 'Market exchanges need a framework of law to operate effectively, the law providing a peaceful way of resolving disputes among parties to a transaction, on the one hand, and, on the other, providing for the punishment of bad behaviour in the market.' Most multinational companies today are very strict in expecting their employees to unequivocally obey the law. Yet despite fairly stringent punishment laid out in, for example, the Foreign Corrupt Practices

Act of the US government, dharma failures are common in the business world.

Aside from dharma and artha, kama, or desire, is a third aim of life. Kama teaches that it is in human nature to want more. Dharma seeks to give coherence to those desires by containing them within an ordered existence. Since no amount of regulation will catch all the crooks who transgress dharma, what is needed in the end is self-restraint on the part of each actor in the marketplace, and this leads to the building of trust. When there is trust in society dharma prevails. Thus, self-restraint on the part of individuals and trust within society are aspects of dharma. At the heart of the market system, Tom Trautmann tells us, is the idea of exchange between ordinary, self-interested human beings, who advance their interests peacefully in the marketplace. In fact, transactions in billions of dollars take place daily in the modern global economy on the basis of trust.

Dharma is the invisible glue of norms and values between transacting persons, which allows them to trust each other and transact with a sense of safety. The best enterprises in the marketplace are aware of this. They tend to build a reputation for dharma-like behaviour, and they are generally rewarded for this. The market system, thus, depends not only on laws but on the self-restraint of individuals, which allows them to cooperate and trust each other in the marketplace. This is how dharma is related to artha. However, there are limits to restraint and trust. This is why the *Arthashastra* instructs the ruler about the importance of *danda*, the 'rod of the state', to punish those who fail dharma.

A concern with dharma is ultimately a concern for duties rather than rights. Unfortunately, today's political discourse in modern democracies is focused mainly on rights, and it seems to me that we have gone too far. The notion of dharma is a good antidote, reminding us that duties underlie rights. Just as one cannot understand America without the idea of liberty, so one cannot understand India without the idea of dharma. The great Sanskrit scholar, P.V. Kane called modern India's Constitution a dharma text, but he too was unhappy with its excessive focus on rights rather than obligations (which underlie those rights). The founding fathers of the Indian republic were so deeply concerned with dharma that they insisted on placing the symbolic wheel of dharma in the Indian flag. This has not, alas, curtailed the pervasive corruption in Indian public life.

1 November 2011   Gurcharan Das
New Delhi

PREFACE

WHEN GURCHARAN DAS invited me to compose a book on the *Arthashastra* for his series I was delighted, for it took me back to a favorite text on which I had written a book and a PhD dissertation a few year ago (Trautmann 1971). The Greek philosopher Heracleitus has said that one can never step in the same river twice. He might have said one can never read the same book twice, not because a book keeps changing like a river, but because the reader changes from one reading to the next. A new reading of a loved book is a deeper reading, and Kautilya's *Arthashastra* has surprised me with many things that were new to me this time around. Partly it is a question of focus. I was to concentrate on its economic aspect, which gave my reading direction and a set of new questions to ask; and it was to be short and accessible, which sharpened the field of vision and kept me from straying into lesser issues. What was commissioned as a work for general readers became, unexpectedly and to my pleasure, a field of new discoveries in scholarship. I thank Gurcharan Das for bringing me this appealing opportunity, and for his support and comments along the way.

The first reader of the manuscript was Robbins Burling, a friend who does an author the kindness of giving comments that are intelligent, blunt and uninhibited. My colleague at the University of Michigan, Tom Weisskopf, who encouraged me to write this book, commented on the first draft, giving me the benefit of his lifelong study of the economy of India. I also got invaluable comments from Mark McClish, whose dissertation on the composition and structure of the *Arthashastra* gives him deep knowledge of the text; from Nadia Sultana Hasan, who gave me the perspective of an economics student; and from fellow author in this series Lakshmi Subramaniam, who gave me helpful comments on the big-picture aspects of the argument. Gurcharan Das fed me thematic suggestions, writings of himself and others useful for this project, and words of encouragement along the way. I thank them all, warmly, for their very great help. I have no doubt the book is better for their criticisms. Readers are not to blame them, however, for the remaining shortcomings of the book, which belong to me alone.

I. INTRODUCTION

THE SCIENCE OF WEALTH

THE THREE LEGITIMATE goals for individuals, according to an ancient doctrine, are kama (love), artha (wealth) and dharma (religion and morality). Each of the trivarga, or group of three, has its shastra. As artha is wealth, *Arthashastra* is the science of wealth. According to this doctrine, the pursuit of dharma is of the first importance, the pursuit of artha is secondary to it, and secondary to both artha and dharma is the pursuit of kama. As it says in the Panchatantra, a book for the education of princes, one should pursue wealth and love as if one were immortal, that is, patiently and persistently, but one should pursue religion 'as if Death himself had seized you by the hair', or, in other words, urgently and intently.[1]

Artha means wealth in all its forms, including money, moveable and immoveable assets but many other things as well. One ancient treatise, the *Kamasutra* of Vatsyayana, defines artha as the acquisition and increase of things as intangible as learning, as personal as friends and as concrete as land, gold, cattle, grain, household goods and furnishings, or, as we might say, intellectual, social and material capital. It advises us to learn about artha from a treatise of royal administration called 'The Duties of Overseers', from merchants and others conversant in economics (vartta).[2]

What is arthashastra?

From its name we would expect arthashastra to be about economic enterprises, but that is only a part of it. In the main, arthashastra is the science of kingship, the business of running a state, specifically, a kingdom (*rajya*). Wealth, here, is identified with kingship. How did that come about? As part of the trivarga, artha means wealth in the extended sense of worldly success which would include political power. These days, economics and politics are demarcated as separate domains, but in the concept of artha, economics and politics were conjoined as a unit. We need to keep this difference in mind while reading the *Arthashastra*. Viewed from a current context, certain parts of the *Arthashastra* seem to be about economics while other sections are more political in nature. But for its original audience, artha was a unitary whole, comprising wealth and power.

In the *Arthashastra* of Kautilya, the author defines wealth in stages, moving from individual wealth to kingship. The fundamental concept is vartta, the closest Sanskrit term we have for the word 'economics'. More precisely, it means the pursuit of livelihood (vritti) or the production of goods, which has three branches, namely, farming, herding and trading. These economic activities produce grain, livestock, money, raw materials (kupya) and labour (1.4.1). Livelihood is the starting point of the *Arthashastra*'s definition of artha:

> The source of the livelihood (vritti) of men is wealth (artha), in other words, the earth inhabited by human beings. The science which is the means of the acquisition and protection of the earth is *Arthashastra*. (15.1.1–2)

In these two compact sutras, artha is defined in three steps—first, as the human production of livelihood, then, as the earth inhabited by human beings engaged in such production and, finally, as the acquisition and protection of the inhabited, productive earth—by a king, we are to understand. Thus wealth finds its highest expression in kingship because kingship involves the acquisition and protection of inhabited, productive territory. By implication, the pre-eminence of the king in artha is grounded in the king's power to tax the productive people living in the territory he possesses.

Just as wealth production has a political character, kingship has an economic character and is conceived as a form of the production of wealth. Although the age of the *Arthashastra* had wealthy merchants and a vigorous international trade in luxury goods, linking India with China and Rome, the ancient Indian science of wealth is about kingship as the apex of economic activity. The underlying logic of this way of conceptualizing wealth is that kingship, with its powers of taxation, had the greatest capacity to form pools of capital to undertake large enterprises such as monumental architecture, empire-building through warfare, diplomacy and maintaining peace in the kingdom. Kingship stands at the pinnacle of wealth formation as it is situated at the pinnacle of society, giving wealth a political dimension. At the same time kingship has economic enterprise at its core. The science of wealth is the science of politics, and vice versa; artha *is* rajya, and *Arthashastra* is its science. This identification of economic power with political power implies that the two are inseparable and are sides of the same coin.

As we shall see in this book, arthashastra is about economic enterprises, both those undertaken by private individuals and those undertaken by the king. But more specifically it deals with the wealth-generating activities of kings, such as the acquisition of territory and the taxation of the people inhabiting it. The king himself ran a highly active economic enterprise. The king taxed farmers but was also a farmer himself, in respect of his own agricultural land. He was involved with the acquisition and care of cattle, horses and elephants, mining, extracting forest products, manufacturing weapons for the army, and the making of cloth on a large scale for the use of the royal family and its servants and also for sale in the market. Thus the kingdom was an economic enterprise, similar to private enterprises, in competition with some of them, in partnership with others. But unlike private entrepreneurs, the king was also the keeper of law and order, taxing and regulating economic undertakings of the people, including farmers, herdsmen, artisans, traders and bankers, and in these matters he was above private enterprise. The relation of kingship and wealth, then, was a complex one, in which the king played multiple roles of entrepreneur, taxing authority, arbiter of disputes and keeper of public order.

The *Arthashastra* of Kautilya

The *Arthashastra* of Kautilya is the oldest surviving text of the science of wealth, the best and most extensive of them. It is about two thousand years old. My goal in this book is to analyse the economic circumstances of the time and the logic of the *Arthashastra*, in the conviction that it has much to teach us that has value in our own times.

This book is intended to be an introduction to the economic philosophy of the *Arthashastra*. It aims to get at the underlying logic of economic action in the text, and to that end I will select particularly revealing examples for analysis. I will sample significant parts of the text rather than reproducing the whole, since my object is to convey the central ideas that will be valuable to us in thinking about our own world today.

The task appears straightforward, but it is not, because the terms we are familiar with today do not exactly match the economic and political concepts of the *Arthashastra*. For example, we have already seen that while we distinguish economics from politics, the *Arthashastra* asserts their unity. That means that if we simply abstract economic aspects of the text and ignore the rest, we will not be true to the logic of the *Arthashastra*.

In order to make this point concrete, let us consider that the *Arthashastra* is divided roughly in two, the first five books dealing with internal administration (*tantra*) and the remaining part devoted to foreign affairs (*avapa*). This would seem to address economics and politics, respectively. The first five books will be most useful for a study of economics, in the sense of vartta, or livelihood or production. However, the remainder of the text, dealing with foreign affairs, is also economic in the sense of being greatly concerned with the relative valuations of various assets of the kingdom (villages, pastures, trade routes, mines, forests) as these should be assessed when deciding on war, concluding peace, or when dealing with an ally. When diplomacy turns into warfare, the king's treasury (*kosha*) is carried in a chest and put under guard in the centre of the army camp.

The whole of foreign policy, therefore, is equally a part of the science of wealth. This will become especially evident in chapter two of this book, when we see the different economic characteristics of kingdoms and republics.

Economists themselves are not entirely unanimous about the definition of economics and what exactly is the object of its study. Both 'provisioning' and 'rational choice-making' have claims to be what economics is about. On the one hand economics is about producing things, about providing human beings with the things they need and want, such as the provisioning of a household or a state. The word economics means householding, derived from the word for house (*oikos*) in ancient Greek. This is the conception with which economics as a science was launched, and political economy meant householding at the level of the state. On the other hand economics is also about a kind of action in which we are obliged to make choices among abundant desires because they exceed our means of satisfying them. Thus economizing is about the rational weighing of objectives under conditions of scarcity.

This book will make use of both ideas, provisioning and rational choice-making. The *Arthashastra* has much to say about the best ways of providing for the requirements of the kingdom. In a sense the king's palace and the apparatus of government is a household that needs supplies, larger in scale but similar to the household of a single family. In that respect the science of wealth is about householding or provisioning. On the other hand, the *Arthashastra* and the tradition to which it belongs values cool analysis of comparative benefits and choice-making among them, which corresponds to the notion of economizing behaviour and the rational calculation of benefits and costs. Thus both approaches to economics are useful to us. The *Arthashastra* speaks in detail of provisioning the kingdom in its chapters on internal administration, and of choosing among various desirable ends in its chapters on foreign affairs.

In this analysis I will treat the *Arthashastra* as a unitary text. The *Arthashastra* describes itself as a compendium of earlier treatises, and various scholars, including myself, have identified features that seem to be later additions by someone other than Kautilya.[3] However, for present purposes it is useful to set such considerations aside and take the text as we find it, as did its readers in ancient times.

Quotations from the text are from the translation of R.P. Kangle, though I have felt free to make editorial changes for greater readability, and have occasionally altered the wording where the Sanskrit original seemed to require it. I refer to Kautilya's text as 'the *Arthashastra*', and the tradition of which it is a part as 'arthashastra'.

What can we learn from the *Arthashastra*?

What can we learn, two thousand years later, from the *Arthashastra* of Kautilya? We learn something about how the economy of ancient times functioned, which is valuable in itself. But does the past teach us anything that we can put to use today, under quite different conditions?

There have been many books and articles written

claiming to draw lessons for today from the *Arthashastra*.
Many authors claim to find in the *Arthashastra* validation
for their favorite economic doctrines, whether of state
planning, free markets, or the latest style of business
management. It is hard to place much confidence in
such claims. The error of that approach is obvious—
state planning, free trade and the latest management
styles are recent phenomena, and the historical
conditions under which the *Arthashastra* was composed
were very different from those of today. Moreover,
approaching the *Arthashastra* to confirm us in what we
already believe may be comforting but it is not very
useful. For we only *truly* learn when what we learn is
something we do not already know or when we unlearn
something we thought we knew. Again, some writers
today treat Kautilya as a sage from whom we can get
timeless wisdom that is true today as it was thousands of
years ago. This does not seem to be a valid way to read
the *Arthashastra*.

These approaches rest on a belief that there is
something eternal or at least durable in economic
phenomena and the conduct of economic enterprises
that holds good over centuries. This way of looking at
things, of course, is not entirely wrong. Human needs
are based on the structure of the human body, which
has not changed much in the two thousand years since

the *Arthashastra* was written. But what we consider to be *necessities* of life has increased and changed with new inventions and discoveries, which means that the process of providing for it is always in a state of motion even if the human body has remained substantially unchanged over millennia. And, after all, provisioning depends not only on what we absolutely need to barely live, but what we desire, in order to live richly. What is constant is that our wants always outrun our means to fulfil them. In a general way, economics deals not with permanent needs but the enduring need to make choices among aspirations that exceed our capacity to supply them all. We can understand the *Arthashastra* because we share a common humanity with its author, but the social, political and economic conditions of its time are so different that we cannot find direct lessons for our time from the text. The error of that approach is that it compresses history. It collapses the long view. But the long view is the very thing that will be useful to us today, because it teaches us something that does not merely confirm what we already know or believe.

Indeed, what we can reliably learn from the *Arthashastra* is virtually the opposite of the supposed confirmation that economic policies of state planning, or of free enterprise, or certain present-day management styles, are valid for all times. What we learn is quite different.

We learn what was the economic policy that accounted for the long success of kingship in its day. And this gives us a point of comparison that can illuminate the very different conditions of the present by contrast. It is the several thousand years of kingship (and not the scant two centuries of British colonialism) that provide us with a point of contrast by means of which we can see our present condition in the long view of history.

In this study of the *Arthashastra* we shall learn a number of things about kingship in India as a generator of wealth—things about kingdoms, goods, workplaces and markets.

Kingdoms (Chapter Two) In the *Arthashastra* there was only one alternative political form to kingship, the sangha or republic. Kingship, by unifying power in a single royal family, was less cohesive than the republic and was vulnerable to overthrow by assassination or by army takeover as the republic was not. However, the economic advantage of kingdoms over republics was substantial and in the long run kingdoms prevailed over republics, and flourished for a very long time. The economic advantage of kingship lay in a vastly superior ability to amass capital through taxation and economic enterprise.

Goods (Chapter Three) Kings, as we see in the *Arthashastra*, required expert knowledge of goods and materials for the successful running of the kingdom, especially the maintenance of the palace and the army and also warehousing of grains and other foodstuff for distribution to the people in times of famine. Kings paid great attention to treasure, in the sense of gold, silver and precious stones as means of diplomacy, warfare and provisioning the royal court and aristocracy. This is very different from the present-day scenario of machine-made, mass luxury goods in the form of consumer durables aimed at a growing middle-class.

Workplaces (Chapter Four) Kingship organized the geographic landscape into a characteristic pattern of economic zones, of which agricultural land was the largest and the most important priority. Other lands were designated for pastures, trade routes, markets, cities and forests. Workplaces were usually located near the source of raw material or in the city near marketplaces to minimize high transportation costs. Forms of labour were of many types and grades, with slavery, bonded labour and some forms of debt servitude at the unfree end of the scale. The most privileged forms of labour were the artisans organized in guilds, who had some level of power in setting the terms of their transactions with customers.

Markets (Chapter Five) Private property and true markets existed, but the overall goal of the *Arthashastra* was to treat extremes of price as harmful to society, both buyers and sellers. Extremes of price were to be countered by intervention of the king's officials. There is an underlying feeling that everything has a proper price and that deviation from it should be policed. The attitude toward merchants was that they have a useful economic function to fulfil, but the king's officials were to be cognizant of the many ways of cheating customers. The trader's profit is conceptualized as a fee for transporting goods to market, and to hike prices beyond fair profit is viewed as an evil to be punished.

The most important finding to emerge from this reading of the *Arthashastra* deals with the ancient concept of the relation of the king to the land and his people. British writers during the period of colonial rule applied Aristotle's idea of Oriental Despotism to India, that is, that the king owned all the land of the kingdom and derived unlimited powers from this ownership, since all citizens of the kingdom were perceived to be his slaves or dependants holding land, not as private property, but by his favour. The *Arthashastra* is a treatise of practical advice about ruling and not a theoretical work on the nature of the king's authority. But while the king is presumed to be able to do much as he wishes within the limitations of his means, a close reading shows the dominant idea is not one of sole ownership but that the king has a share (bhaga) along with other shareholders. The concept of the all-important land tax, upon which the economy of the kingdom mainly relied, being the king's share of the crop, and of the king being the holder of a one-sixth share (shad-bhagin), is a commonplace of the ancient texts. In the *Arthashastra*, the idea of a king's share, and therefore of the king being a co-sharer with the people of the kingdom, appears in connection with taxation, leasing of mines, sharecropping on the king's own agricultural land and in many other contexts. This way of conceptualizing the king's relation to land and people draws upon the idea of the men of a joint family being co-sharers of the family agricultural land, and of partners in economic enterprises holding shares in profits—essentially economic arrangements. This is very different from the notion of unlimited and one-sided power of the king to extract resources and oppress his people at will that is contained in the doctrine of Oriental Despotism.

After I have developed these themes in the chapters to follow, I will make use of them to construct a long view in the final chapter, shedding light on our own times.

The making of the *Arthashastra*

That the *Arthashastra* has survived two thousand years is a sign of the high esteem in which it was held by successive generations. Books in ancient India were copied one by one onto palm leaf or other perishable material. After a time they disintegrated from age, insects and decay. A book would become completely lost if the manuscripts were not copied again and again, as older manuscripts wore out, in an unbroken chain, over two thousand years in the case of this text. Moreover, a book that was considered outstanding in its field had the effect of killing off earlier books it surpassed. The earlier books were no longer re-copied and were eventually lost to later generations. The *Arthashastra* of Kautilya was one of those book-killing books. It was one work of a tradition of knowledge about kingship and quotes by name several previous authorities on the science of wealth, such as Bharadvaja, Vishalaksha, Pishuna, Kaunapadanta, Vatavyadhi and Bahupadantiputra, as well as named schools of *Arthashastra*, the Barhaspatyas, Aushanasas, Manavas, Parasharas and Ambiyas. But none of these earlier *Arthashastra*s have survived. We know that there was an earlier tradition of *Arthashastra*, but we know little of its contents except from what we learn in the surviving *Arthashastra* of Kautilya; the success of the *Arthashastra* of Kautilya had the effect of destroying its intellectual ancestors.

The *Arthashastra* of Kautilya acknowledges in the opening sutra that it was made out of pre-existing *Arthashastra*s. As it says:

This single *Arthashastra* has been prepared mostly by bringing together as many *Arthashastras* as have been composed by ancient teachers for the acquisition and protection of the earth. (1.1.1)

The 'Duties of Overseers' referred to in the *Kamasutra* passage mentioned above as a place to learn about artha seems to have been a self-contained treatise, perhaps one of those *Arthashastras* by ancient teachers which was absorbed into Kautilya's work, because its name is the same as the name of Book Two of the *Arthashastra*. The *Arthashastra* was a synthesis of the science of wealth, so successful that the prior texts from which it quotes ceased to be re-copied and became extinct.

As Benoy Chandra Sen said, the special character of the *Arthashastra* is its focus upon practical economic and political considerations, quite different from the ancient texts on dharma. For example, Kautilya's discussion of the territory of an ideal king 'is not directed by any special religious or racial bias' that divides sacred territories from impure ones when he refers to the southern trade route being superior to the one leading to the Himalayas because it holds more desirable goods, namely, conch shells, diamonds, precious stones, pearls and gold from the south; skins, blankets and horses from the north. The stigma attaching to the southern country in the Baudhayana Dharma Sutra is not in evidence. Moreover the *Arthashastra* shows no moral scruple in organizing the traffic in liquor, 'keeping within prescribed limits, so as to make it a durable and respectable source of income for the State', or when the king has a share of the animals brought to the slaughter-house, 'which flourishes as a normal feature of the country's economy'.[4] Much the same can be said of the *Arthashastra*'s treatment of courtesans and gambling. Liquor, butcher shops, courtesans and gambling are considered quite the norm of kingship and dealt with in a matter-of-fact manner, without moralizing. The king participates in some of these trades himself, taxes them and keeps them from becoming destructive to social order by regulating them.

After the *Arthashastra* of Kautilya, newer works of arthashastra were composed, such as Kamandaka's *Nitisara*, which is virtually a versified abridgement of Kautilya's work. In the *Mahabharata*, the long section called the Shanti Parvan is a kind of *Arthashastra*, and the rajadharma sections of the Dharma Smritis of Manu and Yajnyavalkya contain important traditions on kingship probably borrowed from the arthashastra tradition. But none of the *Arthashastras* after Kautilya's was deemed to surpass it, so it did not fall victim to the success of later works, and continued to be re-copied. Because of its singular longevity, we can say that the *Arthashastra* of

Kautilya has a pre-eminence in Indian civilization that is comparable to that of Sun Tzu's *Art of War* in Chinese civilization, or Machiavelli's *The Prince*, in European.

Nevertheless, although the *Arthashastra* enjoyed a high repute, it had only a narrow readership and copies of it were few. In recent times it had been thought to be lost, until an anonymous pandit brought a manuscript copy of it to R. Shamashastry, librarian of the Mysore Government Oriental Library, who published a translation in 1906–08.[5] The publication caused a sensation among scholars, because of the high importance and rarity of the text and its point of view. Scholars searched for other copies, and a few more manuscripts of the *Arthashastra* were found. Because each hand-copy of a manuscript is likely to result in small errors, and in reproducing future copies there is a tendency for errors to become more numerous over time in any given text, the only way of restoring the original text is to compare manuscripts in order to detect errors introduced by the scribes who copied them. Professor R.P. Kangle produced a critical edition (1960) of the text, that is, a text made after comparing all the manuscripts to infer the original readings and to purge subsequent errors and additions, and at that time he had only seven manuscripts and eight commentaries to work from. That is not many. Compare a widely read text of a similar period, the *Laws of Manu*, for which the existing manuscripts are in the thousands and thousands. From this immense number of manuscripts, Patrick Olivelle selected fifty-three that were largely independent of one another, as well as commentaries and citations of Manu by other authors, as a basis upon which to make a critical edition of Manu.[6]

In the Dharmashastra tradition, the very successful *Laws of Manu* represents a new departure. It creates two new topics not found in earlier dharma texts, the 'Duties of the King' (*raja-dharma*) and the eighteen titles of the law of transactions (*vyavahara*).[7] These new topics of dharmashastra draw their material from arthashastra texts, very possibly the *Arthashastra* of Kautilya itself, but Manu treats kingship in a less practical and a more religious manner. It is possible that the huge success of the text of Manu had the effect of eclipsing the readership for the more detailed, extensive and practical *Arthashastra*. This could account for the small number of manuscripts of the *Arthashastra* compared to those for Manu.

Author and date

What can we say about the author and date of this invaluable text? Both are matters of debate among the experts.

Let us start with the question of what I will call its social location. If we had no information about the author we would nevertheless readily infer from the nature of its contents that the book was composed by a learned brahmin actively working for a real kingdom, not probably as a royal priest (*purohita*) but as a minister (*amatya*) or adviser (*mantri*) on practical, secular matters of administration, diplomacy and war. Since we do know the name of the author, we can confirm from other texts that Kautilya (or Kautalya—the spelling varies) is a brahmin gotra (clan) name. Arthashastra is one of the subjects the prince is supposed to have had recited to him daily as part of his education (1.5.14), so the prince is part of the intended audience. But it was also intended, we must suppose, for the education of the social class of brahmin ministers who produced arthashastras and the would-be ministers who were their sons and their students. It is likely that the previous teachers of arthashastra quoted by Kautilya were of the same social type, and the stream of texts they produced were intended to perpetuate their class and its special knowledge as a preparation for holding office.

This Kautilya, author of the *Arthashastra*, is identified with Chanakya, minister to the first Mauryan king, Chandragupta, and depicted in stories as the brains behind Chandragupta's takeover of the empire of the

Nandas in about 321 BCE. The adventures of Chanakya and Chandragupta are told in a cycle of tales preserved in Hindu, Buddhist and Jain books.[8] These stories are popular entertainment rather than the accounts of eyewitnesses to historical events. For example, in one of the stories Chanakya is said to have been born with a full set of teeth, which was interpreted as a sign that he would be a king; but his pious parents did not want their son to become a king and fall into sin through the violence with which kings are inescapably involved, so they broke his teeth to nullify the prophecy, whereupon it was prophesied that he would become a king concealed within the likeness of a king (*bimbantarika raja*), a kind of puppet-master pulling the strings of kingship, the power behind the throne. Again, in another story it is said that king Nanda was enraged when he saw Chanakya sitting on the king's seat at a royal distribution of alms to learned brahmins, and Chanakya in turn was enraged at Nanda when the king's attendants threw him out of the assembly, and he publicly vowed to destroy the dynasty. When the king's men chased him, Chanakya, thinking quickly, disguised himself as an Ajivika ascetic by the simple expedient of taking off all his clothes and plunging himself into a state of meditation. His later actions as minister to Chandragupta make him the ideal type of the clever brahmin minister and political trickster. We cannot accept these tales as history but there is little doubt that there was a real Chanakya who was a person of great historical importance even if the facts about his life have been turned into folklore.

The big question is whether Kautilya, the author, and Chanakya, the minister to king Chandragupta Maurya, are one and the same. Ancient sources say yes, and one passage of the *Arthashastra* alludes to the defeat of the Nandas by the author, which tends to confirm this identity:

> This science has been composed by him, who in resentment quickly regenerated the science and the weapon and the earth that was under the control of the Nanda kings. (15.1.73)

That would settle the matter in the absence of contrary evidence.

Doubts, however, have arisen over several matters and have become the subject of debate among scholars. An important consideration in the debate is that the text does not make a single reference to Chandragupta or to the Mauryan Empire or its capital city, Pataliputra. The kind of kingdom it presupposes is of modest size, not a huge empire, and the description of it is not strikingly close to what we know of the Mauryan Empire through such contemporary sources as the inscriptions of Ashoka and the memoir of the embassy to Chandragupta of the Greek ambassador from the kingdom of Seleucus, Megasthenes. This is not a fatal objection, however, for, as Kangle rightly points out, advice tendered by the *Arthashastra* is directed to a hypothetical king ruling a hypothetical kingdom, not the real Chandragupta Maurya ruling a real empire.[9] This is the conventional frame of all the arthashastras. Moreover, the content of its advice also comes from the tradition represented by prior arthashastra texts, not from contemporary examples or historical precedents. This argument seems entirely sound; but its effect, unfortunately, is to say that there is no evident linkage between the empire-making work of Chanakya and the text-making work of Kautilya, which is the opposite of what we would expect. Moreover, it diminishes the value of the *Arthashastra* as a source of historical information about the Mauryan Empire. It is like the cure that kills the disease but also, unfortunately, kills the patient.

There are specific elements in the text which seem to require a post-Mauryan date. It would not be appropriate in a book of this kind to list them all, but I will mention one general pattern that I consider very telling. The *Arthashastra* pays a good deal of attention to luxury goods, including goods coming from as far away as China and Rome. Although it does not speak of the trade with these places directly, it mentions some of the precious commodities that derive from it. As to China, it speaks of China silk (*china-patta*). The name for China did not come into use until the Chin dynasty, starting in 221 BCE, that is, long after Chandragupta Maurya and Chanakya. As to Rome, the Roman trade with India grew rapidly in the first century CE or slightly earlier, long after the Mauryan Empire had broken up, when Greek sailors at Alexandria, then under Roman rule, learned how to use the monsoon winds to carry their ships from the Red Sea to India and back in a short time. The volume of that trade as we will see (Chapter Three) was tremendous, and there was a large flow of Roman gold and coral to India and of Indian gems and pearls to Rome. Connected with that trade and the same time horizon, the *Arthashastra* mentions the red coral of the Mediterranean, greatly prized for the making of jewellery, coming from Alexandria. It uses the rare name Parasamudra, 'across the sea', for Sri Lanka, datable to the first century because it is picked up by Greek sailors of the time, as Palaisimoundou. And it speaks at length of the pearls of south India, which would be consistent with Roman testimony to the large export of pearls from south India and Sri Lanka to Rome in this period (first–second centuries CE). We know that the Roman trade picked up China silk in Indian ports as well. All of this favours a date of about 150 CE for the *Arthashastra*, rather than the time of the Mauryan Empire (321–175 BCE).

Eminent scholars, however, looking at the same evidence can come to diametrically opposed conclusions. For example, Kangle, whose knowledge of this text was unsurpassed, favoured a Mauryan date, whereas S.R. Goyal, one of India's pre-eminent historians of the ancient period, who made a close comparison of the *Arthashastra* with the account of the Mauryan Empire by the contemporary Greek ambassador, Megasthenes, concluded that the evidence proves the date of the *Arthashastra* is post-Mauryan.[10]

Whether the *Arthashastra* is a text of the Mauryan period or of the post-Mauryan period, over which scholars disagree, most agree that it is the product of a tradition containing different schools of thought and notable teachers, and that some elements of the tradition go back a long way, even *before* the Mauryan Empire. For example, an old doctrine of arthashastra is that there are four means (*upayas*) to which the king should resort when dealing with another state: conciliation (*sama*), gifts (*dana*), sowing dissension or 'splitting' (*bheda*) and force, including war (*danda*). Kautilya undoubtedly found this doctrine appearing in the previous texts of the tradition. The *Arthashastra*, by its own account, is not a description of a specific actually existing kingdom, but a synthesis of prescriptions about the practice of kingship in general made, perhaps over centuries, by many teachers, whose business was to advise the king in the running of the kingdom.

2. KINGDOMS

ARTHASHASTRA IS THE science of wealth and, at the same time, the science of politics, specifically of kingship. Economic power and political power are inextricably connected and the king is the highest embodiment of this.

Kingship has been the dominant political form in India and in the world for thousands of years, a dominance that is only now coming to an end. Kingdoms have been replaced by representative democracy—the modern avatar of the ancient republic—as the norm for political life. The independence of India and Pakistan marked an important step in that process, ending the last vestiges of kingship with the winding up of the Indian princely states. It also opened the floodgates of decolonization that created an abundance of new nation-states out of the European empires. The winding up of kingship in Nepal in 2009 brought to a close the last Hindu kingdom in the world. The only kingdom to have survived in the subcontinent is Bhutan. Kingship is slipping into the past before our eyes. Because arthashastra is about wealth and kingship at one and the same time, in order to understand the ancient science of wealth we will have to understand the nature of ancient kingship. Understanding kingship will help us better understand the nature of its successor, the modern republic.

The *Arthashastra* tells us about kingship in a twofold manner: first, in a direct manner, by its advice to the king on all aspects of ruling his state, and second, by comparison with what it says about what normative kingship in its day was *not*—the republic.

Ancient republics

The *Arthashastra* distinguishes two models of political organization, the kingdom (*rajya*) and the republic (*sangha*). It devotes a whole book, Book Eleven, to republics. We know that republics had a long history and some were very successful, lasting for centuries and even issuing coinage in their own names. Some of them were conquered and made tributary states by powerful kingdoms, while others held their own against kingdoms

that attempted to conquer them. Using what the
Arthashastra says about republics, from the point of view
of the king we can throw into sharper relief the character
of kingdoms as states and as economic enterprises.

We begin with what the *Arthashastra* says about the
overall aspect of the republic as seen from the viewpoint
of the king:

> The gain of a republic is the best among gains of an
> army and an ally. For, republics being closely knit are
> unassailable for their enemies. He should win over
> those of them who are friendly with conciliation
> (sama) and gifts (dana), and those hostile through
> dissention (bheda) and force (danda). (11.1.1–3)

Thus republics are formidable as enemies and armies
because they are closely knit, and by implication,
kingdoms are less closely knit and less unassailable.
Why is that? In a republic, political power is broadly
spread across a warrior class, whose members debate
and decide public affairs in assembly. Because decision-
making is shared, strong solidarity among the
stakeholders is generated, and each member of the class
takes responsibility to advance the well-being of the
whole. The greatest asset of the republic is the strong
cohesiveness that grows out of this sharing of power. It
has a direct payoff in inculcating a strong fighting spirit

and military effectiveness, as the *Arthashastra* attests. At the same time, and in contrast with kingship as we shall see, its tendency is more defensive than offensive.

The French sociologist Émile Durkheim (1858–1917) distinguished two types of social solidarity. In a simple society, without much internal differentiation of functions, the solidarity that holds society together is based upon the high degree of *likeness* among people making up the society. Durkheim calls this pattern 'mechanical solidarity'. In a more complex society, the division of labour creates many economic specialist groups which, because they are not self-sufficient and have to exchange their goods and services, are interdependent. Durkheim calls this pattern 'organic solidarity'. These terms indicate that Durkheim thought complex organic societies had a stronger solidarity than simple mechanical ones. But the reverse was true in Kautilya's view, and the *Arthashastra* contradicts Durkheim's theory by upholding the strength of the republics, which were prime examples of mechanical solidarity.

The ancient republic or sangha was based upon the likeness to one another of members of the ruling warrior class, and the differentiation of social groups by economic specialization (division of labour) was limited in the republics though not entirely lacking in some. The

Arthashastra distinguishes two different kinds of sanghas, the second of which is more socially complex than the first:

> The Kambojas, Surashtras, Kshatriyas, Shrenis and others live by agriculture and warfare. The Licchivikas, Vrijikas, Mallakas, Madrakas, Kukuras, Kurus, Panchalas and others live by the title of raja. (11.1.4)

The first kind is made up of peasant–warriors, and we can imagine them as largely self-sufficient and having few servants or slaves. The second, however, speaks of a warrior class who call themselves rajas, and we can surmise they were landowner–warriors with servants and slaves to till the land for them. Such a twofold social system recalls a Buddhist text that speaks of republics consisting of rajas and dasas (slaves), rather than the four castes of brahmins, kshatriyas, vaishyas and shudras. Here the social system is complex, in the sense of having permanent classes with different functions and statuses, but less complex than the system of castes associated with kingdoms. Also, we note the presence of multiple rajas in such a republic. In a sense, the republic is not the *absence* of kingship but the *pluralism* of kingship, and we could say that the single sovereign (ekaraja) concentrates the several rulers of the warrior class of the republic into one family line ruling a kingdom.

Although the republic had a certain sense of shared equality within the warrior class, it was not a democracy like the modern republic of India, in that political rights were not extended to all. The republics were socially simpler than the kingdoms, which were closely linked to the four castes (*chaturvarnya*). The caste system in consonance with Durkheim's theory is in part a division of labour involving both the differentiation of groups by economic function and their economic interdependence. Kangle speculates that the deliberative assembly of republics was made up of the heads of clans, and that seems most likely and reasonable.[1] We can assume the clans were held together by intermarriage, and the allied clans as constituting a people sharing a common name.

We do not know the constitution of the republics in any detail. Unfortunately, the *Arthashastra*'s treatment of republics is from an external perspective. The main thrust of Book Eleven is not to explain the workings of republics but to advise the king on how to overcome a hostile republic, attacking the solidarity of its warrior class by the device of sowing dissension among them, and so weakening the whole. We do not learn a great deal about the political and social structure of the republic from it. Since the great teachers of Buddhism and Jainism came from republics, and some features of the constitutions of the political structure of ancient republics are contained in the rules governing the Buddhist and Jain orders of monks and nuns, some information on the republics can be culled from these religious texts. Significantly, as a throwback to the republics from where these two religions started, their monastic orders are called sangha.[2]

Ancient kingdoms

The differing social structures and statecraft norms of republics and kingdoms had political and economic ramifications. Republics could engage in territorial expansion, but they do not seem to have had an inherent tendency to expand without limit and form empires, because they were based upon the 'mechanical solidarity' of likeness and this social mechanism posed limits to their ability to absorb conquered peoples as slaves or dependents. Republics did form confederacies with other republics, which was another means for enlargement, but it seems there were inherent limits to that process as well, in that the larger the number of members of a confederacy the more difficulty it had holding together. While kingdoms conquered and ruled over republics, the opposite did not happen. To cite an instance, the Shakya republic, from whose ruling, warrior class the

Buddha came, lost its independence to the aggressively expanding kingdom of Kosala. Kingdoms did not just annex neighbouring territories through military offensive, they also employed clandestine means to achieve the same result. Magadha was an expanding kingdom rivalling the larger Kosala at the time of the Buddha and the Mahavira. To the north of Magadha was the state of the Vrijjis of Videha, a confederacy of tribal republics from where Mahavira came. Stories about King Ajatashatru of Magadha show him as ruthless and aggressive. Unable to defeat the Vrijjis across the Ganga to the north, he faked a quarrel with his brahmin minister, Varshakara, who pretended to flee for his life and took refuge among the Vrijjis. There he sowed dissension among them, making them vulnerable to conquest and absorption by Magadha. This story is not a contemporary eyewitness account but it is a dramatic embodiment of arthashastra teachings, including the policy of fomenting internal conflict to undermine the solidarity of republics. Varshakara embodies the type of secular brahmin minister who like Chanakya and Kautilya were the authors and perpetuators of the arthashastra tradition.[3]

Kingdoms, then, seen in the contrasting light thrown on them by the republics, had less social unity and greater social complexity. Political power was not spread broadly across the warrior class, but concentrated in a single lineage, that of the royal family. Kingdoms had a complex division of labour, which enhanced their economic power. They had an unlimited urge to conquer, expand, absorb and tax foreign populations and to acquire virgin lands and settle them with tax-paying agriculturists. Kingdoms, because of their centralization, had a greater capacity to mobilize money, form ever larger armies, build magnificent palaces and temples, and preside over an increasingly hierarchical social order. Luxury goods from distant lands played an important role in defining and maintaining that hierarchy as acquisition of these items was dependent on the economic status of people which in turn was linked to the social and political power they wielded. Kingdoms were economically active and dynamic in ways the republics were not.

Accompanying these advantages of kingdoms were a number of enduring problems related to the political structure that could be managed but could never be solved once and for all. The first of these was that since all power was concentrated in an individual, the kingdom was vulnerable to being taken over simply by killing the king, a problem which did not exist for republics, making them much more difficult to defeat. Because of this vulnerability to assassination, the *Arthashastra* shows great concern for the security of the king's person, especially with regard to the layout of the palace, which was provided with defences and hidden passageways for escape. Snakes and poison are two objects that mark the *Arthashastra*'s attentiveness to security, and it conveys useful lore about the detection of both. Poisoning and poison-detecting birds are especially associated with kings and kingdoms:

> The parrot, the starling or the fork-tailed shrike shrieks when there is fear of snakes or poison. In the proximity of poison, the heron becomes frantic, the pheasant becomes faint, the intoxicated cuckoo dies, the eyes of the chakora bird become discoloured. (1.20.7–8)

The king was vulnerable to rivals of all kinds, and even his own brother, son or wife. For this reason the concentration of power in a single royal family places great strains upon family relationships, especially the closest ones. The king is at his most vulnerable when making love, as we see in the following passage:

> In the inner apartments he should visit the queen after she has been cleared by old women. For, concealing himself in the queen's chamber, Bhadrasena was killed by his brother, and Karusha was killed by his son, concealed in his mother's bed.

> The king of Kashi was killed by the queen, mixing
> fried grain with poison under the guise of honey;
> Vairantya was killed by the queen with an anklet
> smeared with poison; the king of the Sauviras with a
> poison-smeared girdle-jewel; Jalutha with a poison-
> smeared mirror; Viduratha was killed by the queen
> who concealed a weapon in the braid of her hair.
> (1.20.14–16)

Thus the king's most intimate relations are sites of the
greatest potential danger to his life.

The relation of the king to his son was especially
fraught with suspicion and conflict. The *Arthashastra*
devotes a whole chapter to 'guarding against princes',
while another chapter advises the prince in disfavour
how to conduct himself, and the king how to deal with
him (1.16, 17). The king–prince relationship was
evidently an abiding concern, because the *Arthashastra*
recites the teachings of prior authorities on how the
king should manage the prince. Kautilya rejects the
advice of each of the previous authorities as being
ineffectual or dangerous. Prescriptive methods
recommended by earlier authorities for keeping in line
wayward princes included inflicting silent punishment
on the prince (Bharadvaja), confinement of the prince
to one place (Vishalaksha), making him reside in the
frontier fortress (the Parasharas), or in the fortress of a

distant prince (Pishuna), or with the kinsmen of his mother (Kaunapadanta), allowing him to indulge in vulgar pleasure so as to not become hostile to his father (Vatavyadhi). Kautilya considers the last prescription a 'living death' and a danger for the royal family. His formula for controlling an errant prince recommended the exact opposite, namely participation in religious rituals and education in practical affairs by experts (1.17.22–27).

The *Arthashastra*'s prescription for education of the prince included training in the expert knowledge necessary for the running of the kingdom, which would include *Arthashastra*, but the greater stress was put on learning personal virtue and self-control. Secret agents of the king should present themselves to the prince as his friends and guide him on good paths, and keep the king informed. The prince should not be subjected to tests of loyalty, as are the king's officials, which would be a dangerous course as it would sow ideas of distrust and rebellion which were hitherto unknown to him.

> 'And one of the secret agents should tempt him with hunting, gambling, wine and women, saying "Attack your father and seize the kingdom." Another should dissuade him from that.' So say the Ambhiyas.
>
> This awakening of one not awake is highly dangerous, says Kautilya. A fresh object absorbs

whatever it is smeared with. Similarly the prince,
immature in intellect, understands as the teaching of
the shastra whatever he is told. Therefore, he should
instruct him in what conduces to dharma and artha,
and not what is harmful. (1.17. 28–30)

The argument that tests of loyalty risk the 'awakening
of one not awake' and so create a danger that did not
previously exist identifies the problem with such tests
generally in the search for trust, a scarce and valuable
quality in a kingdom.

Finally, since kingdoms had large armies under a
centralized, unitary command, and concentrated
armouries, there was always a possibility of a military
takeover in a way that simply could not occur in the
republics, in which the fighting force was dispersed in
peacetime and weapons were privately owned. There is
a tradition that the last Mauryan Emperor was killed by
his general, Pushyamitra, while reviewing the troops.[4]
Pushyamitra then formed the successor state, that of
the Shungas. Because of the danger to the king from the
concentration of army power, the *Arthashastra*, speaking
of the military force assigned to a fort, says that there
should be *several* commanders, to provide checks and
balances to avert coups (2.4.29–30). In this case the
concentration of royal power in a single leader was
protected by *dividing* military power among several

leaders. A whole chapter of the *Arthashastra* is devoted to dangers from conspiracies among the king's own appointed officials (9.5).

Besides the danger to the king's life, the very ability of the kingdom to amass and concentrate wealth required a large establishment of royal servants, who then had opportunities for peculation. The *Arthashastra* has some vivid metaphors to express the inherent difficulty of detecting misappropriation of money:

> It is not possible *not* to taste honey or poison placed on the tongue; just so, it is not possible for one dealing with the money of the king *not* to taste the money, if only a little. We cannot know when a fish *swimming* in water is *drinking* water; just so, we cannot know when officers appointed for carrying out works are appropriating money. It is possible to know the path of birds flying in the sky, but not the ways of officers moving with their intentions concealed. (2.10.32–34)

In one notable passage the *Arthashastra* lists forty different kinds of embezzlement (2.8.20–21), most of them having to do with falsification of accounts. Embezzlement is only one of many sources of loss to the treasury discussed in the text under the topic of 'Recovery of revenue misappropriated by officials' (2.8). Detecting misappropriation of the king's wealth by his own servants was a constant preoccupation. Throughout the text on appointed officials and their duties the *Arthashastra* speaks of the keeping of accurate written records. But record-keeping, necessary as it was for the functioning of the complex enterprises of the kingdom, did not do away with the problem and, indeed, offers an additional means by which misappropriation could be hidden.

Because his servants did not work under his direct supervision the king needed to find people he could trust. The *Arthashastra* gives a great deal of attention to tests of trustworthiness, especially of the higher officials such as ministers and generals—tests of religion (dharma), material gain (artha), lust (kama) and fear (bhaya) (1.10). As these tests of loyalty involved agents who propose disloyal action and offered some kind of temptation in order to provoke a telling reaction, the tests themselves carried a degree of risk. The constant worry about trustworthiness has to do with the concentration of power in a single ruler. At bottom, concentration of power in a single ruler created fear of assassination in the king and temptation of assassination for officials, creating an atmosphere of distrust in which loyalty was always tentative and subject to sudden change.

Officials, in order to gain favour, were likely to tell the king what they thought he wanted to hear. The ruler therefore had a countervailing need for sources of candid information about what was taking place in his kingdom. The *Arthashastra* therefore advises the creation of a large establishment of spies working under various disguises and operating in several different ways. Spies working in various guises—student, wandering monk or nun, farmer, trader, religious hermit, poisoner or fighter—were on the payroll to gather information for the king. In part the spy establishment was simply the information-gathering arm of the kingship, much like the *harkaras* or personal news-gatherers who were employed by all high officials and wealthy traders in the Mughal period and indeed almost to the beginning of the nineteenth century. Thus in one aspect the spy establishment was simply the 'information order' of kingship, using the term of historian Chris Bayly about the routines of gathering information necessary to running the kingdom.[5] But spies did not merely gather information, they also initiated activities to promote a favourable attitude toward the ruler among the people, and sometimes to do the king's dirty work in the form of 'silent punishment' and other shadowy actions.

Because of all these vulnerabilities flowing from the concentration of power in his hands, the king needed to provide for the ultimate catastrophe in which he has to flee the kingdom in haste:

On the border of the country, he should cause a permanent treasure (*dhruva-nidhi*) to be buried by persons condemned to death, as a provision against calamity. (2.5.4)

What happens to those condemned prisoners is not said, because it does not need to be said. They are killed. The value of this buried treasure is that it is secret.

Thus kingship had a very considerable downside and its superior ability to amass and concentrate wealth was accompanied by inescapable costs. A short list of them includes the cost of providing security to the king; the strains upon relationships within the royal family, especially with the sons and the queen, sometimes resulting in murder of the king; danger of army takeover; loss to the treasury due to the peculation of officials; and the cost of maintaining the spy establishment. None of these costs were borne by republics, so in this respect the kingdoms were at a disadvantage, and their treasury was drained by ongoing unproductive costs. However, the greater powers of kingship must have outweighed these costs and the vulnerabilities that drove them, because in the long run the republics succumbed and kingdoms flourished. The historic success of kingship as a political form implies its superior economic power compared to that of the ancient republics.

A historical example may give a sense of the level of

the advantage of kingship. The Greek historians of Alexander's expedition to India give us examples of a republic in the Punjab, and the empire of the Nandas, which they simply called the Easterners (Prasioi, Sanskrit Prachya). Of the republic, the historians say that it had 5,000 councillors (that is, leaders of the republic) each of whom brought an elephant to war to defend the state; in other words, the warrior class that made up the deliberative assembly owned the means of warfare as individual property, including war-elephants, which they brought to the national defense. The Nandas, on the other hand, are credited with having huge numbers in the military—2,00,000 soldiers, 20,000 cavalry, 2,000 chariots, 3,000 or 4,000 elephants.[7] Now it has often been remarked that the Greek writers had a motive in exaggerating the size of Indian forces in both cases, particularly of the Nanda kingdom as the soldiers of Alexander mutinied and refused to advance further into India; exaggeration served to excuse the soldiers of cowardice. And the numbers are incredibly large. But, whatever the true number of each taken separately, they probably do reflect the comparative advantage of kingship over the republic.

This impression is confirmed by Megasthenes' embassy to Chandragupta Maurya. Megasthenes paints a vivid picture of the Mauryan military machine, in which he evinced great interest. According to his accounts the military formed the largest class after agriculturists, and was centrally paid, while the farmers were unarmed and not subject to military service. Armies were employed for offensive and defensive action while the farmer, undisturbed, tended his fields and flocks nearby in perfect peace. Arms, horses, elephants and chariots were the property of the state and housed centrally. It appears that the Mauryas were continuing policies of the Nandas in these respects.[8]

The economic base of that large, unitary and expensive military was taxation. This achieved folkloric expression in the figure of Dhanananda (Wealthy Nanda), who deposited a fabulous lost treasure in the Ganga—possibly a never-used dhruva-nidhi or permanent treasure for emergencies.[9]

The two species of political form, kingship and republic are traceable back in time, and aspects of both are found in the earliest texts of the Vedas, from about 1200 BCE. Deliberative assemblies are commonly mentioned, and political power was broadly diffused across the kshatriyas, the warrior class. It was only gradually that the concentration of power in a single royal family developed in some of the tribes, while others retained the tradition of shared decision-making powers. In that process, the Vedic religion of sacrifice developed by Brahmins was very much on the side of kingship, and deployed its rituals of royal consecration to the task of lifting the king above his peers and the members of his own extended family with ceremonial enactments of competitions such as games of dice or chariot races, through which the king won at the expense of warriors (*rajanya*) or family members. Arthashastra is connected with the Vedic tradition of supporting kingship, although through practical and secular advice, not through ritual, and in some places indicates its adherence to the Veda.

Accordingly, the ideal of kingship for the *Arthashastra* of Kautilya is called the life of a rajarshi, a king who is a rishi or sage (1.7). This means control over the senses—casting out lust, anger, greed, pride, arrogance and foolhardiness. It means leading a life of self-control in the midst of luxury. And it means a life of constant labour and attentiveness to business.

The daily round of the king was rigorous to an extreme. The king's days and nights were each to be divided into eight parts (I will call them hours for simplicity's sake, but each one is equivalent to an hour and a half of our hours) by the sundial and the water clock. This was the king's daily schedule:

First hour of the day, listening to military measures and accounts;

second hour, considering the affairs of the city and country;

third hour, bath, meal, study;

fourth hour, receiving revenue and assigning tasks to the overseers;

fifth hour, consulting the ministers and studying the information gathered by spies;

sixth hour, recreation or consultations;
seventh hour, reviewing elephants, horses, chariots and soldiers;

eighth hour, deliberating on military plans with his commander.

He would then worship the gods in the evening twilight. This was the king's schedule for the night-time:

First hour of the night, interview secret agents;
second hour, bath, meal, study;

third, fourth and fifth hours, sleep;

sixth hour, awaken, study the shastra and preview the work of the day;

seventh, deliberate with councillors and dispatch secret agents;

eighth hour, receive blessings from priests, gurus, purohita (chaplain), see his physician, chief cook and astrologer.

> And after pradakshina (circumambulation) round a
> cow with calf and a bull, he should proceed to the
> assembly hall. (1.19.25)

This exhausting schedule allowed only four and a half
of our hours for sleep. We cannot believe such an ideal
was ever followed in practice. Thankfully, there was
room for relaxation of this demanding pace:

> Or, he should divide the day and night into different
> parts in conformity with his capacity and carry out
> his tasks. (1.19.26)

Even so, his day and night were highly structured and
filled to the brim with work. The life of a king was not a
life of pleasure and ease. It was a life of hard work and a
kind of asceticism amid unparalleled wealth. It reminds
us of the concept of non-attached action in the Bhagavad
Gita, acting without attachment to the fruit of action,
living in the world and performing the duties of one's
social condition while remaining unmoved by the
rewards of action, living in the world but not swept
along by it.

3. GOODS

KINGSHIP REQUIRES DETAILED and expert knowledge of goods and the raw materials from which they are made, for provisioning the palace and the army as also for distributing food to people in times of famine. In this chapter I will draw up an inventory of storehouses and goods in the *Arthashastra*, in order to infer its underlying scale of valuation. The valuation pattern underlying the provisioning process is king-centric, in the sense that it pays greater attention to treasure and less to common goods; treasure being necessary for diplomacy, warfare and for sustaining the social pre-eminence of the king and the aristocracy.

The longest and most interesting of the fifteen books of the *Arthashastra* is Book Two, 'Duties of Overseers' (*adhyakshas*); overseers are the heads of the different government departments. It is also perhaps the most difficult to read, because it contains an abundance of practical details concerning different types of materials and the technical aspects necessary for their acquisition and processing. In short, it has the kind of information one would get from professional experts rather than from writers of literature, and uses technical vocabulary rather than literary prose. Hence there are many terms in Book Two that are obscure to us because they are given in lists without any explanation and are not found in other works of Sanskrit literature from which we might been able to discover their meanings. (Many words whose meanings are uncertain are left untranslated by Kangle.) This is a fair indication that the author of this book culled his knowledge from living experts in the various branches of material production and did feel the necessity to explain these terms. It is here that the practical side of the *Arthashastra* is most evident.

Individuals and states alike have to provision themselves, acquiring, storing and replenishing stocks of food, clothing, shelter and commodities needed for daily life. We can see the kind of goods an ancient kingdom needs in order to subsist by analysing the *Arthashastra*'s discussion of the duties of the director of stores (*samnidhatri*). His duties include building well-constructed storehouses of different types and providing for receiving, evaluating and dispensing goods.

The first and most important of the storehouses is the *koshtagara*. Kangle has used the term 'magazine', but 'granary' would seem a better translation, as koshta means grain, keeping in mind, however, that a variety of foodstuff was stored there, not just grain. Secondly, there is the storehouse for 'forest products' (*kupya-griham*). Thirdly, there is the armoury (*ayudhagaram*) and, finally, the treasury (kosha or *kosha-griham*), which includes objects of great value. These are the main storehouses but there is also a passing mention of the storehouse for goods (*bandhagara*), the room for merchandise and medicine (*panyaushajya-griham*), and pens for cattle and stables for horses and elephants in the city or in the fort. Strangely, the director of stores was also to build a prison house (*bandhanagaram*), perhaps because he possessed knowledge of constructing strong and secure storehouses, or because prisoners had to be provisioned from the granary.

We will make an inspection tour of the granary, storehouse of *kupya*, armoury and treasury so that we can draw up an inventory of the goods needed to provision the kingdom and get a sense of the relative valuations of different commodities that comprise the total stock. Viewing the stock of goods as a totality will make evident the relative valuations of things making up the stock. The items that figure prominently in the text will be those that are valued highly. What is absent from the stock will also be important information about what is taken for granted. I will then analyse selected items of the inventory, which are specially revealing about the structure of the economy, namely pearls and red coral; textiles and pottery; horses and elephants.

The granary

The granary has its own overseer (*koshtagara-adhyaksha*). The granary stocks come from the king's own farms, under the supervision of the overseer of royal farmland (*sita-adhyaksha*), and probably also from produce in lieu of land tax, which is under the care of the administrator of revenue (*samahartri*), from farmers working their own lands. The inventory of the granary includes grains, such as two varieties of rice (*shali* and *vrihi*), grains (*kodrava*, *priyangu*, *udraka*, wheat, barley and sesame); two kinds of beans (*mudga* and *masha*); fats, such as butter, oil, suet and marrow, different forms of sugar such as treacle, jaggery, unrefined and refined sugar; different forms of salt such as fossil salt and sea salt, *bida* salt, saltpetre, borax and salt from salty soil; sweet liquids, including honey and grape juice. There are also fermented drinks of sugary liquids or fruit juices and spices, possibly made on the premises by the staff; sour liquids such as curds and sour gruel; spices such as long pepper, black pepper, ginger, cumin, bitter *kirata*, mustard, coriander; spices of whose identity we are not certain called *choraka*, *damanaka*, *maruvaka*, and *shigra* stalk (but not the chilli pepper, which came much later from the Americas); and dried foods such as fish, meat, roots, fruits and vegetables. The granary holds a large and variegated stock of foodstuff.

No doubt every farming family in the villages had its own granary as did every grain merchant in the city. In that sense, the king's granary was simply a larger version, serving a larger household. But the king's granary had the additional function of providing relief to people in times of famine:

> From his granary the king should set apart one half
> for the people in the countryside in times of distress,
> and use the other half. And he should replace old
> stock with new. (2.15.22–23)

'Distress' (*apad*) indicates that preparations must be in place for unexpected exigencies at all times. It also indicates that the king's granary in ordinary times does not supply the public or issue foodstuffs at subsidized prices as the modern welfare state does. The two purposes of the royal granary are to supply the royal household (palace and army) and to alleviate distress during famine. The *Arthashastra* does not give us details about actions, for example, whether, in times of distress, foodstuffs were distributed free or sold. But the bare prescription that one-half the granary is kept aside for relief measures shows how very uncertain the food supply was in ancient times, and how critical it was for kingdoms to alleviate the plight of the people during periods of severe food shortage. Possibly the ability to do so was another advantage of kingdoms over republics.

The granary overseer has to know the different kinds and qualities of the different foodstuffs, the kind of taxes to be levied, marketing, weights and measures and the keeping of accounts. He has to supervise the staff in the protection, movement and processing of the stock and the issuing of rations. The staff includes the sweeper, watchman, weigher, measurer, supervisor of measuring, dispenser, delivery supervisor, receiver of tallies, slaves and labourers. Grains are stored in the hull and are milled in the premises, as needed. Other processing is undertaken as well. For these purposes the granary is equipped with tools of several kinds: implements for weighing and measuring, grinding-stones, pestle and mortar, pounding machine, oil press, fan, winnowing basket, sieve, cane-basket, box and broom. (2.16.62–63)

Milling, oil-pressing and other processes bring about changes in volume of foodstuffs, and the overseer of the granary has to be conversant in the ratios at each stage of processing so as to have continuing control of the inventory.

> He should personally observe the quantity by which
> grains increase or decrease when pounded, rubbed,
> ground or fired, moistened, dried or cooked. (2.15.24)

Examples of changes in volume through processing are then given. Thus, in both varieties of rice, the substance when milled is one-half of the grain in the hull, before it is milled. Of priyangu, the substance is one-half plus one-ninth; of udraka the mass is the same, also in wheat and barley when pounded, and sesame, barley, mudga and masha beans when rubbed. In legumes, the substance is one-half, in lentils, one-third less. Oil extracted from pressing linseed is one-sixth, from sesame, one-fourth. And so forth. These changes in volume have to be understood and tracked so that the total quantity of inventory items is known at all times.

We then come to the issuing of foodstuffs for the palace and the army.

Processing foodgrain results in food of fine or coarse quality. While issuing rations there are two implied criteria: finer quality for animals and humans of higher order, and the quantity proportional to the size of the recipient (greater quantities for larger bodies). The overseer therefore has to be conversant with the standards.

As to the quality of rations, better milling yields less but better rice from a given volume of paddy. For example, from five *dronas* of paddy, if milling yields twelve *adhakas* of low-grade husked rice, it is suitable for feeding a young elephant; if milling yields eleven adhakas, it is suitable for a mature elephant; if it yields ten adhakas, it is suitable for riding elephants; if nine adhakas, it is for war elephants. For soldiers, if it yields eight adhakas; for chiefs, if it yields seven adhakas; for queens and princes, if it yields six adhakas; for kings if it yields five adhakas—'or one *prastha* of rice-grains, unbroken and cleansed' (2.15.42). Broken grains are reserved for slaves, workers and cook's helpers, and lesser animals such as ducks, geese, goats, sheep and cattle (2.15.62, 52–56). (It is hard to determine the exact size of these measures, and Kangle does not render a translation. The actual size of measures is not important in the present context, in which we are trying to get at the logic of the provisioning process.)

As regards the quantity of rations to be issued to inmates in the king's household: for upper-caste (Arya) males, the measure is one prastha of rice, one-fourth prastha curry (supa), salt one-sixteenth of the curry and butter or oil one-fourth of the curry. For lower castes the measures are less. It is one sixth prastha of curry, and half the butter or oil. For women the measure is less by one quarter, and for children, it is less by one half. Thus ration units are proportionate to the status of the person and the body size. Proportions for preparing curries with meat and with vegetables are given; for twenty *palas* of meat, the appropriate measures of fat, salt, sugar, spices and curd are mentioned; for vegetable curry, the ingredients are one and a half times the quantity it is for meat; for dried meat, the ingredients are twice the quantity it is for meat. We are not to presume that the granary staff cooks these meals, but they use the proportions and rations given in the text to calculate totals when issuing (uncooked) provisions for the army, the royal kitchen and for the elephant and animal stables. For example,

> The horse-attendant shall receive from the treasury and the granary a month's allowance (for the horse) and carefully look after it. (2.30.3)

Both the horse-attendant and the overseer of the granary need to have these model daily rations in mind in order to calculate the volume of each item for a given period of time.

When it comes to the rations for elephants, the amounts are large, and ruinously expensive for the owner. It is costly to maintain an elephant in a stable in the fort or in the city; it is far cheaper to let it feed itself by grazing in the countryside. The ration for an elephant stabled in the fort is calculated on each cubit (aratni) of the elephant's height. The ration is one drona of rice, half an adhaka of oil, three prasthas of butter, ten palas of salt, fifty palas of meat, an adhaka or two of juice to moisten dry lumps, an adhaka of liquor with ten palas of sugar or twenty of milk as an invigorating drink, a prastha of oil to smear on the limbs, one eighth that for the head and for the lamp; and then, two and a quarter loads (bharas—a large amount) of grass and two and a half of hay; and, 'of leaves of plants and so forth there is no limit.' (2.31.13)

For a horse stabled in the fort or city the ration is also large. For the best breed of horse, two dronas of rice or barley or priyangu, half dry or half-cooked, or half-cooked beans (mudga or masha) and a prastha of fat, five palas of salt, fifty palas of meat, an adhaka of juice or two of curds to moisten the lumps, a prastha of liquor with five palas of sugar or ten of milk as an invigorating drink (2.30.18). We see that the underlying pattern of the ration for horses is the same as it is for elephants, but the quantities are less. The horse-ration mentioned above is reduced by one quarter for a middling breed of horse, and one half less for the lowest breed. The ration for horses is the pattern followed for bullocks, to which is added one drona of masha or a pulaka of barley; the special ration is one tula of oil-cake from the press and ten adhakas of broken grains and bran. Rations for buffaloes and camels are twice the quantity for bullocks; it is half a drona for donkeys, spotted deer and red deer. Rations are stated for two kinds of deer (*ena* and *kuranga*), goats, pigs, dogs, swans, herons, and peacocks (2.25. 51–59).

> For deer, beasts, birds and wild animals other than these, the Overseer should cause an estimate to be made from one meal consumed by them. (2.15.59)

These animals are of the palace grounds or in the wild animal reserves maintained by the king.

Thus, the ration for an elephant is used as a model but varied in quantity depending on the size and breed of horses, cattle and other animals. There is also a model ration for humans which is modified for persons of different status. The pattern of model ration and variation for different cases is the manner of exposition for the *Arthashastra*, but it is also an indication of how the overseer of the granary calculates quantities in the course of his work of the issuance of rations, keeping track of the inventory and receiving new stocks of goods of every kind every working day.

The store of kupya

We now turn to the function and duties of the overseer of kupya (*kupya-adhyaksha*). What is kupya? Kangle translates it as 'forest products', because the first sutra of the section on his duties says that the overseer should have guards to bring kupya from produce forests (or forests for materials, *dravya-vana*). That translation fits the items of kupya that are listed, with one exception, namely the metals, iron, copper, steel, bronze, lead, tin, *vaikrintaka* (an alloy of some kind) and brass (2.27.14) which come from mines rather than from forests. Mines have their own overseers which are different from the overseer of kupya. Note, by the way, that the list of metals omits the precious metals such as gold and silver. The dictionary definition of kupya is 'base metal'. Evidently kupya includes but is not limited to forest products. It is something like 'building materials' or 'raw materials', just as kostha is not just grain, but foodstuff in general. We will stay with the Sanskrit word itself, given that there is no English word which covers the meaning of the term. Readers should keep in mind that kupya includes forest products, covering metals other than gold and silver, and denotes materials that do not fall in the category of precious goods.

In addition to the non-precious metals, then, this is the inventory of the kupya store, derived from the forest for materials, in outline: hardwoods (twenty-one varieties are named in the text); reeds (eight varieties); creepers (five varieties); fibre plants (seven varieties); rope fibres (two varieties); leaves (three varieties), flowers (three varieties); medicinal plants (four categories); poisons (sixteen varieties) as also poisonous snakes and insects (the whole constituting the group of poisons); and the following body parts of animals:

> Skin, bones, bile, tendons, eyes, teeth, horns, hooves
> and tails of the lizard, *seraka*, leopard, bear, dolphin,
> lion, tiger, elephant, buffalo, *chamara*, *srimara*,
> rhinoceros, bison and *gavaya*, and also of other species
> of deer, beasts, birds and wild animals. (2.17.13)

We will see in a moment what these body parts are used for. The list continues with the non-precious metals already mentioned; baskets and pots made of split bamboo-cane and clay (that is, baskets and pots; please note for future discussion); charcoal, husks and ashes; pens for deer, beasts, birds and wild animals; and warehouses for fuel and grass.

The armoury

The chapter on the duties of the overseer of the armoury (*ayudhagara-adhyaksha*, 2.18) immediately follows the duties of the overseer of forest products, the first of several indications that there is a close connection between forest products and warfare. For example, in the fort there is provision for the storage of both weapons and kupya. As the armoury contains implements for war and weapons, we may say that kupya is the raw material and the armoury contains implements related to war made from kupya. It is also includes armour made from hides and other body-parts of animals in the passage mentioned above.

The overseer of the armoury has to supervise the making of arms, armour and accoutrements of war and their safe storage. The inventory begins with fixed machines of ten named varieties, all of them colourful but obscure for us, for example, the 'many-headed', the 'kill-all', the 'arm', the 'half-arm'. These are followed by mobile machines, which include the hammer, mace, spade, trident and discus among the sixteen named varieties. Then come weapons with piercing points (eleven named varieties); bows (seven varieties, including bows of wood and horn); bowstrings (six varieties, including sinews), arrows (five varieties, with tips made of iron, bone or wood); swords (three varieties); hilts (made of rhino or buffalo horn, tusk of elephant, wood or bamboo root); razor-type weapons (seven varieties); stones (four varieties); coats of mail (made of metal rings or plates), an armour of fabrics, 'and combinations of skin, hooves and horns of dolphin, rhinoceros, *dhenuka*, elephant and bull'; shields for the arm and for other parts of the body (sixteen varieties).

It is evident that kupya was mainly acquired as a source of raw material for the military. But we cannot presume that is the whole story as products made from kupya served other important needs too. Iron, for example, has many peaceful uses, and in some ways it is the most important of metals, though in the *Arthashastra* we hear only of artisans working on gold and silver, and the minting of silver and copper coins. We are now aware that the pattern of exposition in the *Arthashastra* is to give a model for the normative or standard use, and secondary uses follow this model, with suitable alterations. This pattern suits the sutra style of exposition, which values brevity, but it also follows the style of practical reasoning used by the experts in calculating quantities for the provisioning process. Sometimes the secondary uses are left unspecified.

The treasury

The overseer of the treasury (*kosha-adhyaksha*) is in charge of the receipt of 'gems, articles of high value, articles of small value or kupya' (*ratnam saram phalgu kupyam va*) into the treasury and presides over bureaus of experts in the various lines (2.11.2). Ratna in this chapter has both the broad sense of treasure and the more specialized sense of a gem, so that ratna (gem) is one of the items of ratna (treasure). The chapter on the duties of this overseer concerns the receipt of precious goods or treasure (ratna), and addresses the three items of ratna (in the narrow sense of gems), sara and phalgu, leaving kupya to the section on the overseer of kupya. This, therefore, is a section on luxury goods. The inventory is as follows:

Ratna: pearl, ruby, beryl, sapphire, diamond, red coral

Sara: sandalwood, aloe, incense

Phalgu: furs and skins, woolen cloth, silk cloth, cotton cloth

I will not go into all the detail which the *Arthashastra* gives on these items, but I will examine pearls and coral later in this section. Pearls get first place in the discussion here as they are described in greater detail than any other item in the inventory. The text speaks first of the origins (entirely in India), defects and excellences of pearls. The primacy of pearls in the text, and the incredibly large numbers of pearls in necklaces that it speaks of, are significant indications of the large role of pearls in ancient Indian life and, as we shall see, the importance of Indian and Sri Lankan pearls in Rome as well. The *Arthashastra* names five varieties of pearl strings, and then the kinds of necklaces made from multiple strings, beginning at the top of the hierarchy with the Indracchanda of an astonishing 1,008 strings, followed by necklaces of 504, sixty-four, fifty-four, thirty-two, twenty-seven, twenty-four, twenty and ten strings, each with colorful names, and finally the *ekavali*, or a single string. We may wonder whether a necklace of 1,008 strings of pearls ever actually existed, but even if it did not, it signifies that the conception of the largest imaginable necklace, serving as a standard of measure for all lesser necklaces, was very large indeed.

The text then describes necklaces with different kinds of strings and with gems and gold ornaments. These descriptions apply also to 'strings and networks for the head, hands, feet and waist'. The volume of pearls mentioned in the text is astonishingly large. The series of ratnas ends with red coral, coming from Alexandria in the Mediterranean. The extensive treatment of pearls and the mention of coral is probably because of the large luxury trade with Rome in the first and second centuries CE, a matter to which we shall return.

The inventory of precious goods in the treasury lacks the precious metals gold and silver, and also coins. That is not because the treasury did not have them but because they are discussed, at some length, in other chapters. Gold is discussed in chapters immediately following, on mines, on the overseer of gold in the king's workshop and the royal goldsmith in the market highway (2.12–14). Coins and the mint are also discussed elsewhere, under the rubric of standardization of weights and measures (2.29).

This completes our inventory of goods in the *Arthashastra*. The advantage of having drawn up the inventory is that it gives us a perspective of the whole. As we can see, it is very much the point of view of the king and not of the ordinary person, and it leaves out some very useful objects, such as kitchen knives, plough points of iron or water pots made of clay from the picture, and concentrates on articles of high value which are necessary for displaying the primacy and magnificence of the king, for conducting state-to-state relations and for the military.

I will now select a few goods for analysis that will tell us about various aspects of the economy. We will examine three pairs of goods: pearls and coral; textiles and pottery; horses and elephants. Each is a pair of a different kind, and each tells a different story: the first of luxuries, the second of necessities of life and the third of the sinews of war.

Luxuries: pearls and red coral

Certain goods become luxuries not only because they have intrinsic properties that humans find attractive but because they perform important social functions, singling out their owners as distinguished from others who lack them. The use of luxuries as social markers began long before the advent of written records. The making and trading of beads and other articles of personal adornment go way back into prehistory. But the advent of kingship enhanced the demand for luxury goods and gave it a new role in a new social structure. Kingship ordains that the king will be signified as the apex of the kingdom by his possession and display of precious objects in a superlative degree, which distinguishes him above other wealthy men. The king in this way sets a standard which others would emulate in a lesser degree, especially the higher officials of the king and the aristocracy.

The demand for luxury impels long-distance trade, as buyers are willing to pay a premium for what is both appealing and rare, bearing the very high cost of transport in ancient times. Until the invention of steam engines and other new technology using fossil fuels which drove transportation costs way down in the nineteenth century, trade which involved very long distances was structured around luxuries. From the time of the *Arthashastra* till the beginnings of steam-powered manufacture and transport, that is, for almost two thousand years, the structure of India's luxury trade with the rest of the world was, in its broad outlines, very stable.

Certain objects tend to become luxuries because they are desired, and are desired because they confer distinction on their owners by their rarity and costliness; and among these are objects that come from afar. For this reason, it is in the inventory of precious goods, and not in the granary, or the store of kupya, that we find goods of foreign origin. Red coral is an outstanding example.

India had coral which it has used as a source of lime from ancient times, but the red coral in the treasury is found in the Mediterranean Sea, and is entirely absent in the waters of India and its neighbours. The *Arthashastra* says it is from Alakanda, which is Alexandria in Roman Egypt (2.11.42). Vivarna, the other country named as a source for red coral, is unknown, but it must also be in the Mediterranean region. Red coral is highly prized in India today and continues to be imported. It has become one of the nine gems (nava-ratna) which have special astrological significance and beneficial properties for the health and fortune of those who own and wear them as jewellery. India, then, has depended for thousands of years on imports of this non-indigenous product from coral fisheries thousands of miles away, and continues to do so today. No other country has India's passion for red coral.

The twin of the red coral is the pearl. South India and Sri Lanka have abundant pearl fisheries, especially in the Gulf of Mannar, which were in production in ancient times as the *Arthashastra*'s discussion of pearls implies. From the north Indian viewpoint of the *Arthashastra*, pearls, coming from south India, are a foreign import and a leading item which makes the trade route to the south preferable to the trade route to the Himalayas. Moreover the pearl oyster is found in south India but not found in Mediterranean Europe which makes Indian pearls an item in long-distance luxury trade in the reverse direction, from India to Rome.[1] This trade reached Rome in a trickle through intermediary traders until a few decades before the beginning of the Common Era, when two things happened to create an enormous growth of the luxury trade between India and Rome. First, Rome created an empire that engulfed Greek-ruled Syria and Egypt, from the time of Augustus, and second, Greek seamen of Alexandria and from other Egyptian ports learned the technique of using the seasonal winds of the monsoon to sail across the open waters to India, which lessened an otherwise very long journey along the coast to one of only forty days. India and Roman

Egypt, and therefore Rome itself, were suddenly much closer, and a huge jump in the volume of trade in luxuries ensued. The quantum leap in the volume of trade was facilitated by larger ships. Lionel Casson shows that ships of Roman Egypt were much stronger and larger, up to 180 feet long, than previous ships, so as to withstand the buffeting winds of the south-east monsoons which made the voyage more dangerous but much quicker, and that they carried very large and costly cargoes.[2]

In this trade, pearls and red coral played leading roles, moving in opposite directions. This is a remarkable equivalence, since both come from living organisms in the sea, harvested by divers in waters shallow enough not to require artificial supplies of air, but having territories separated by a long distance, joined by traders using sailing vessels.

Both pearls and red coral appear in the *Arthashastra*'s discussion of gems (ratna), and we find both in the *Natural History* of Pliny (23–79 CE), written in Latin.[3] Pliny's testimony is valuable in that it directly links Roman coral with Indian pearls. He says that gems of coral are prized by Indian men as much as large Indian pearls by Roman women. Before the Romans discovered the Indian love of coral, the people of Gaul (what is now France) ornamented their swords, shields and helmets with coral, but in Pliny's day it had become so scarce because of the price it commanded on the Indian market that it was rarely seen anymore in its native place. He goes on to say that Indian soothsayers and seers consider coral a powerful amulet for warding off dangers, so that it is considered both an object of beauty and one with religious powers. This brings to mind that red coral is one of the nine gems that have beneficent powers and astrological significance to this day. Coral merchants, Telugu-speakers of Balija caste, are leading citizens, prominent in the affairs of nineteenth-century Madras. They are dealers in red coral and pearls, bringing together in the present day the two main luxuries of the ancient trade of India and Rome.[4] In the case of coral, an exotic product from faraway Europe has become an integral part of Indian life and culture, and has remained so for the past two thousand years.

Pliny also tells us that pearls were imported from India to Rome in large numbers and had become the leading marker of opulence. He considered the mania for Indian pearls and other luxuries excessive and destructive of civic values and the wealth of the empire. Pompey had his portrait rendered in pearls, the emperor Gaius wore slippers sewn with pearls, and the emperor Nero had sceptres, actors' masks and palanquins adorned with pearls.[5] Other such outbursts against the excesses of luxury connected with the India trade are found in Pliny's book.

Warmington, summarizing the trade, says that Rome paid for Indian pearls with amber, copper, lead, coral and coined money.[6] The volume of this flow of coined money to India was great: Pliny reckoned it, at a minimum, as 100 million sesterces, a very large figure, to India, the Seres (Cheras of south India, perhaps) and Arabia, 'so dearly do we pay for our women and our luxuries'.[7] The result is large hoards of Roman gold and silver coins in south India and Sri Lanka which have been discovered in the last two centuries. Roman coinage therefore was circulating in Indian marts. Indians minted coins in silver and copper and took up the minting of gold coins when the Roman gold coins became debased by the admixture of cheaper metals under later emperors. The coinage of the *Arthashastra* is in silver and copper, but not in gold, which is consistent with a date for the text of about 150 CE.

For these reasons the *Arthashastra* is best dated in the period of the Roman–Indian trade, that is, the first and second centuries of the Common Era. The very words for coral (*pravala*, *vidruma*) and silk cloth (*kausheya*, china-patta) are absent from earlier Sanskrit texts, such as the Veda and the grammars of Panini and Patanjali, and are first attested in Sanskrit texts of the Common Era, that is, of the period of the Roman–Indian trade.[8]

Daily necessities: textiles and pottery

Textiles and pottery make a pair of a different kind—a pair of opposites. A benefit of making an inventory of goods in the *Arthashastra* is that it allows us to see what is *absent* from the list, or at least just barely mentioned. Scholars have not mentioned before how little we hear of a common commodity in the *Arthashastra*, namely, pottery. By contrast, another commodity of daily use gets prominent mention, namely, textiles. Why is that? Why are these necessities of life so differently valued by the author of the *Arthashastra*? The question has not been asked before. We may not be able to give a definite answer, but we can at least give a partial one.

Cloth and vessels of pottery are human inventions of long ago that have since become necessities of life. In that way this pair of goods differs from the previous one. People can live quite well without pearls or coral, but they cannot live without clothing made of textiles and vessels of clay or some other material. But goods that are necessities of life may also be raised to the level of luxuries, if they are made of costly material and fineness of craftsmanship. In the *Arthashastra*, textiles appear both as necessities of daily life and as luxuries, while pottery does not appear in the inventory of luxury goods, and indeed it barely appears at all.

The *Arthashastra* lists pottery in the inventory of kupya, non-precious raw materials, together with baskets, in a single, short sutra: 'Vessels (are) made of split-bamboo cane and of clay (mrittika)'. (2.17.15) A trivial mention of baskets and pottery does not mean that these were rare, but quite on the contrary they were so common and inexpensive they were taken for granted. Pottery is one of the most common of craft productions of ancient India, so abundant that wherever there has been a long history of settlement one has only to look at one's feet to see uncountable masses of broken bits of pottery lying around on the surface of the land. Because of its abundance and durability, pottery is of inestimable value to archaeologists, who establish chronologies for their sites of study by sequences of pottery varieties. Yet this necessary and useful article finds only one direct mention in the inventory of goods, under the name of the material from which it is made, as an item of kupya: clay. The low value placed on pottery is indicated in another passage of the *Arthashastra*, in which earlier teachers are quoted as saying, about the law of inheritance, that those without property will divide even water-pots (3.5.23), using pottery as a metaphor for a thing of the smallest imaginable value. Of course a water-pot may fetch a meagre market-price but it is a fundamental necessity of life, as necessary to life as the water it contains. The prices of things and the value we place on them do not always correspond to our real needs.

It is not obvious however why pots should have been so little valued in the *Arthashastra*. Pottery can be made with artistry and be objects of connoisseurship by the well-to-do. This happened in China, Japan and Korea and in many other places as well. China had imperial potteries and a large export trade. Shipwrecks of Chinese vessels reveal that whole shiploads of trade pottery were being transported to distant countries. India itself imported some Chinese pottery in medieval times when there was little export of Indian pottery. India had its own luxury pottery at certain periods, notably the brightly painted, appealing pottery of the Indus Civilization, and the Northern Black Polished ware from about 500 BCE, was traded all across north India and to some extent into the south as well.[9] It is possible that the advent of metals drained some of the value from pottery to utensils made of metal. Possibly, growing attention to the doctrine of impurity (*ashaucha*) and the belief that clay goods retain impurity led to a decline of eating from vessels of pottery in favour of banana leaves. Whatever be the reasons, we note it as a problem for further exploration that the value of pottery was decidedly low in the *Arthashastra*, lower than the archaeological record of earlier periods.

Textiles, by contrast, are prominently mentioned in the *Arthashastra*, from two different angles. They appear in the inventory of luxury articles in the treasury, including as we have seen, China silk. And they appear in descriptions of the spinning and weaving operations run by the king's officials, both for the use of the royal household and for sale at a profit, while fulfilling the king's obligation to support widows and orphans by employing them in spinning. We will further explore the striking difference in the valuation of pottery and textiles in the next chapter.

Sinews of war: horses and elephants

The king takes great interest in animals, wild and domestic, in acquiring furs and skins (considered luxuries) and other body parts (considered kupya, non-precious raw materials for the making of armour and weapons, among other things), as has been explained earlier.

Horses and elephants are of high value to the king because they are essential for the army. The ancient army was considered to be *chaturanga*, meaning a four-legged animal, the legs consisting of infantry, cavalry, chariots and elephants. The game of chess was invented in India. It is also called chaturanga, and had four pieces (one of which became a bishop when it reached Christian Europe), in addition to the king and the minister (now the queen). Thus the strategic significances of horses and elephants in ancient India continue to be acknowledged in the present-day chess set.

Horses and elephants form a pair in terms of their use and high valuation, but they pose very different problems of supply the king must address. The differences hinge on the fact that while wild elephants are indigenous to India, wild horses are not. Consequently the problem of obtaining the one animal is quite different from the other. By and large, horses were acquired by trade from Central Asia or countries to the west of India. Elephants were most plentiful in the eastern, central and southern regions of India. In other words, horses and elephants are complementary in distribution. Within India, horses thrive in the more arid regions where there are grasslands, mainly the Indus region and the interior of the peninsula; elephants thrive where there are forests, mainly the forested areas of south India, central India, Orissa (whose kings called themselves Gajapati, 'Lord of Elephants'), Bengal and the north-eastern hill states.

The names of the three grades of horses in the *Arthashastra* are very telling. They are distinguished by their place of origin, the best coming from Kamboja (upper Indus on the Pakistan–Afghanistan border), Sindhu (lower Indus), Aratta (Punjab) and Vanayu (Iran or Arabia); the middling breeds from Bahika (Balkh, ancient Bactria, in northern Afghanistan), Papeya (location uncertain), Sauvira (along the Indus) and Titala (location uncertain); while 'the rest are inferior' (2.30.29). The modes in which the king acquires horses are listed in the opening sutra of the chapter on the duties of the overseer of horses (*ashva-adhyaksha*):

> The Superintendent of Horses is responsible for registering the total number of horses, received as gifts, acquired by purchase, obtained in war, bred in the stables, received in return for help, stipulated in a treaty or temporarily borrowed, according to their pedigree, age, colour, marks, class and source. (20.30.1)

Thus the acquisition and transfer of horses is only partly through markets, and many transfers are state-to-state transfers due to war or diplomacy. Horse-ownership is highly politicized. Because horses are not found wild in India (there are some wild relatives of the horse, but they were not domesticated for warfare), they are imported in all ages, they are expensive, and they are therefore virtually monopolized by the king and the warrior class as privileges of their status and for military use.

The case of elephants is entirely different.[10] Elephants being indigenous, the king is advised to establish an elephant forest (*gaja-vana*, distinct from the materials forest, *dravya-vana*) and acquire them in the wild. Apparently the abundance of elephants in the wild is such that any given kingdom may have them in its territory. Elephants are captured wild, tamed and trained for work and war, but they are not domesticated from birth. The main reason for this mode of acquisition is purely economic. Elephants are prodigious eaters and do not reach the age at which they can be used for human purposes until twenty years, so it is far cheaper to capture them as adults rather than rear them from birth and feed them in stables.

Elephants too come in different grades of quality as do all the items in the inventory of the kingdom. Like horses, different breeds are identified with different regions of origin, but all of them are in India.

> Elephants from the Kalingas and the Angaras are best. Those from the east, Cedi and Karusha, from the Dasharnas and the Aparantas are considered of medium quality among elephants. Those from the Surashtras and the Pancanadas are declared to be of the lowest quality among them. Of all these, valour, speed and spirit increase by training. (2.2.15–16)

The quality (and probably quantity as well) of elephants declines from east to west, the best coming from Orissa (Kalinga), the poorest from Punjab (Pancanada)—where they are no longer found. The geographical horizon of this passage is of the northern parts of India, but another passage suggests that elephants were acquired by trade both from the Himalayas in the north and from the south (7.12.22–24; see chapter five).

The primacy of elephants in warfare is made plain by the *Arthashastra*:

> Victory in battle for a king depends principally on elephants. For elephants, possessing very big-sized bodies and being capable of life-destroying activities, pound the troops, battle-arrays, fortresses and camps of enemies. (2.2.13–14)

Thus, elephants are necessary for military success. But so are horses.

It is a paradox of India's history that the Vedic people brought to India a style of war based on horses, in the form of horse-drawn chariots and cavalry. For India has no true horses in the wild, and until the advent of mechanized warfare in recent times this style of war has been sustained by a steady flow of imported horses from foreign regions, mainly Central and Western Asia. This pattern persisted till the twentieth century, though

the British made the pastures in New South Wales in
Australia a source for horses, known as Walers, for the
army in India. The acquisition of horses is a matter of
high strategic importance and an economic problem of
some complexity for every king.

More manageable, though no less costly, was the
problem of acquiring elephants. But on the whole India
was self-sufficient in elephants and an exporter of these
animals to other countries under the Mauryans, mainly
to the Greek kings of Syria, the Seleucids.[11] Seleucus
concluded a treaty with Chandragupta by which he
ceded the greater part of what is now known as
Afghanistan and the Indus valley to the latter and received
500 elephants in return. This shows the high value that
was placed on elephants and their importance in
diplomacy. From then on, the Mauryans were a source
of elephants for the Seleucids. It is notable that this is a
king-to-king transaction, not a market exchange. The
Greek kings of Syria (the Seleucids) and Egypt (the
Ptolemies), who were rivals, sent emissaries to the
Mauryas, no doubt seeking elephants for the wars
between them. The account that survives of
Megasthenes' embassy under Seleucus shows a great
interest in Indian techniques of capture and training
elephants. This elephant-trade at the level of king-to-
king relations also included the men who possessed

skills to be elephant drivers because the Greek word for an Indian (*Indios*) acquired the specialized meaning of elephant-driver. Subsequently, the Ptolemies and the Carthaginians used Indian techniques to capture and train African elephants, and the Carthaginians took a body of elephants across the Alps to attack Rome. The failure of that venture largely brought an end to elephant warfare in the West. The Romans used military elephants, but were too far removed from the source of Asian elephants to continue for long (but they invented the circus and its association with the elephant, which continues to exist around the globe). During the fourth and the third centuries BCE there had been to the west of India a kind of arms race brought about by the Greeks involving Indian war-elephants. The use of war elephants was also adopted by the Indianized kingdoms of Southeast Asia, as a part of the Indian model of kingship.

As we can see, the king-centred inventory of goods in the *Arthashastra* has a very definite structure, oriented to luxuries and items of high value for war, diplomacy, and the maintenance of the royal household, and taking for granted cheap but necessary articles such as pottery and baskets. A merchant-centred inventory of that period, if we had one, would almost certainly have a very different structure, oriented to the marketplace rather than to the royal household, offering a different array of goods. There appears to have been a far-flung trade in elephants, as they are mentioned in connection both with the trade route to the Himalayas and to the south, but the *Arthashastra*'s treatment of the division of the countryside into economic zones assumes that an elephant forest can be set up in the king's own territory and will not need to be acquired by trade. Because of this decidedly royal point of view, the *Arthashastra* gives us a picture of the economy that is different from one we might glean from a text whose author wrote from another point of view, such as that of a merchant, or from an archaeological dig. It is not a neutral record, but a picture with a purpose and reveals a lot about the economics of kingship.

4. WORKPLACES

DRAWING UP AN inventory of the goods discussed in the *Arthashastra* has given us a means of getting a sense of the scale of valuation that drives the economic policy of the ideal kingdom. In this chapter I will follow a similar strategy by drawing up an inventory in the workplaces at which goods are produced. What we will see is that kings arranged the land they inherited or acquired into different economic zones to provision the royal household and to defend the kingdom. Workplaces are not concentrated in cities (although there were some workshops there) but are mostly near the sources of raw materials, in the different economic zones, due to the high cost of transport in the age before the advent of steam power. This is very different from the present age of machine-based mass production in large factories, in factory towns or cities which house large workforces.

We will also be examining the workforce itself, and the kind of labour which ranged from slavery and debt servitude to wage labour and skilled artisans organized in guilds. This pattern too is different from what we find in our own day, in which slavery and debt bondage have disappeared but in which artisan labour organized in guilds has mostly become extinct and the system of wage labour predominates.

The topography of production

The topography of production in the *Arthashastra* is not determined by the natural features of the landscape alone, but in combination with human objectives and improvements in different modes of transportation. To a considerable extent, the landscape of the ideal kingdom is *made* by human labour, actively shaped at the direction of the king to supply products the kingdom requires. This moulding of the land is brought out clearly in the chapter 'Settlement of the Countryside' at the start of Book Two, in which the king is to provide for farms, pastures, and trade-routes, corresponding to the three branches of vartta or the production of livelihood, and also mines and forests. Generally speaking, the king is to be an active agent in shaping what nature and history have given him by way of territory. The distributed nature of production provides that the ideal territory is one with a variegated landscape.

First among the economic zones of the landscape are the farms. The great strength of the kingdom is its capacity for capital formation through taxation, by which it surpassed individuals and private firms, and other political forms, such as republics. The bulk of economic enterprises being family farms, the bulk of taxation is levied upon agricultural crops. As we shall see, the farming village was the norm for human life in the *Arthashastra*, and a model from which every other mode of life is a kind of deviation. One consequence of the central importance of farming is that the kingdom as an enterprise is oriented toward land and away from the sea; and more specifically it is oriented toward agricultural land inhabited by industrious farmers. This is the root of the king's wealth. It is virtually the opposite of the view of the merchant, for whom the largest profits lie in the luxury trade with distant lands across the seas.

In this chapter we will look at the places of work: farms, pastures, mines, forests and workshops for gold and for cloth. We will conclude with a look at the workers who work in them.

Farms

Because of the prime importance of agriculture for the wealth of the kingdom, Book Two of the *Arthashastra* opens with 'the settlement of the countryside'. It is as if the kingdom began with newly conquered land suitable for farming, either already populated or untilled and unpopulated. This is a useful fiction by which to establish that the first business of the kingdom is farming, and to devise ways to turn empty land into wealth-producing and habitable land. From the beginning the *Arthashastra* makes it clear that the king not only levies taxes on farmers but is actively engaged in increasing the extent of farmed land to increase the kingdom's wealth, thereby enlarging the tax base. Just to be clear, the all-important 'land tax' is actually a tax on the crops, not the land itself, and it takes the form of a king's share (bhaga) of the crop.

> He should cause settlement of the country, which
> had been settled before or which had not been settled
> before, by bringing in people from foreign lands or
> by moving people from overpopulated regions in his
> own country. He should cause villages to be settled
> consisting mostly of Shudra farmers with a minimum
> of one hundred families and a maximum of five
> hundred families, with boundaries extending over

one krosha or two kroshas and affording mutual protection. (2.1.1–2)

The emphasis on shudras as desirable farmers, rather than a landed warrior aristocracy of kshatriyas, for example, is striking. It gives the impression of a separation of farming and warfare, and of a direct relation between king and farmer, unmediated by a landlord class. This is considered ideal from the king's point of view, but often not achieved in practice. Besides giving land to farmers, the *Arthashastra* goes on to say that the distribution of lands should include tax-free grants to brahmins (Brahmadeya) in their capacity as priests, preceptors, chaplains and Vedic scholars, and to government servants, such as overseers and accountants, and to cowherds, *sthanikas* (heads of groups of villages), elephant-trainers, physicians, horse-trainers and couriers. However, most of the land goes to farmers.

At a distance from this normative human landscape, the king appoints chiefs in frontier forts to guard the gates of the kingdom. The territory along the borders and outside the farming zone is to be guarded by tribal people who live in the forest and not in the villages habited by farmers (2.1.5–6).

It is worth remarking that the king is advised to positively attract farmers to his kingdom from foreign countries, and to move people from overpopulated regions of the kingdom to new farms. The policy shows a desire to expand the extent of farmed land, and implies an abundance of land that can be turned to agriculture—a policy oriented toward the countryside and the farming village. The underlying demographic conditions have changed dramatically in recent times. The policy of the *Arthashastra* contrasts strongly with the main demographic fact of the past century, the shift of population from country to city, away from farming and toward factory work due to city-based industrial production. Clearly India was not heavily populated in the time of the *Arthashastra*, even though its population was large for the time, and overpopulation of the countryside has only become a problem for government in quite recent times.

In discussion of the distribution of land to farmers the emphasis is on the connection between possession and paying of tax:

> He should allot to tax-payers arable fields for life. Unarable fields should not be taken away from those who are trying to make them arable. He should take away fields from those who do not till them and give them to others.

We see a very direct relation of the king to farmer, without the intervention of absentee landlords. Farmers have only life interests in fields that have been given by the king, but it appears that these life interest contracts eventually become hereditary, because in other passages of the *Arthashastra* we find that farmers have true private property rights in their lands, being able to sell, mortgage and bequeath. We will explore the matter of private property in the next chapter.

The king not only allots fields to new farmers, he supplies the things they need to bring them under cultivation for the first time.

> He should favour them with grains, cattle and money which they should repay later at their convenience. And he should grant them favours and exemptions which would cause an increase to the treasury, but avoid such as would cause loss to the treasury. For a king with a small treasury swallows up the people of the city and the people of the countryside. He should grant exemptions at the time of settlement or as people come. He should, like a father, show favours to those whose exemptions have ceased. (2.1.13–18)

The king promotes agriculture by caring for the farmers as a class, with a paternalistic mix of kindness and discipline, advancing land, seed, and so forth, but taking back land that is not tilled and has stopped yielding tax. The primacy of the land tax for kingship is evident.

Besides promoting farming and farmers the king is a farmer himself, on a large scale. The king's own farmland, called *sita*, is under the care of the overseer of royal farmland (*sita-adhyaksha*).

> The Overseer of Royal Farmland, conversant with the practice of farming, water-divining and the science of rearing plants, or assisted by experts in these, should collect in the proper seasons, seeds of all kinds of grains, flowers, fruits, vegetables, bulbs, roots, creeper fruits, flax and cotton. He should cause them to be sown in land suitable for each, which has been ploughed many times, through serfs, labourers and persons remitting their fines through personal labour. And he should see that their work is not delayed by ploughing machines, implements and bullocks, and on account of the work of artisans such as smiths, carpenters, basket makers, rope makers, snake catchers and others. If they fail to create the product through their negligence, the fine shall be equal to the value of the product. (2.24.1–4)

We see from this that the king's own farming operations are complex, starting from the collection of seeds for crops and carried out by labourers of different kinds and artisans with various skills. The duty of the overseer of royal farmland is to coordinate, oversee and discipline a large and complex body of labourers. Land is worked by labourers who are paid a wage, or let out to landless cultivators on terms of share-cropping, that is, the sharing of the harvest between the king and the cultivator on agreed terms. The text does not specify what these shares are. But note for later discussion this concept of sharing between the king and producers of different kinds, both parties, however unequal in power, having shares (bhaga) and being in a partnership relation. The *Arthashastra* has many instances of this concept, as we shall see.

There is considerable detail in this chapter that seems to come directly from the practical knowledge of farmers rather than from books. Here is a passage that is an example of that. It concerns the treatment of seed, and it has all the signs of knowledge passed down by practice and oral instruction in the vernacular from one generation to another of farmers, gathered and rendered into writing in the learned language by an interested non-farmer:

> The treatment of seeds of grain is soaking in dew by night and drying in the heat by day for seven days and nights; for three or five days and nights for seeds of pulses; smearing at the cut with honey, ghee and pig fat mixed with cowdung for cuttings that serve as seeds; smearing with honey and ghee for bulbs; smearing with cowdung for stone-like seeds; and in

> the case of trees, burning in the pit and fulfilment of (the trees') longing with cow bones and dung in season (when they send out buds). And when they have sprouted, he should feed them with dried fish along with the milk of the *snuhi* plant. (2.24.24–25)

According to a common folk belief, trees have cravings (dauhrida) that must be fulfilled when they are about to sprout buds, like the cravings of an expectant mother.

Thus the king is strongly identified with farming, as he is a farmer among farmers, albeit on a grander scale than the farmers, who moreover are mostly Shudras. The family farmer is the norm for productive humans who are at the heart of the kingdom. At the same time the king rules over farmers and extracts a tax from them which is the largest source of wealth for the kingdom.

Pastures

The settlement of farmland comes first. The next chapter is 'Disposal of Non-agricultural Land' (2.2), the title of which tells us that all other economic zones are secondary to farmland. Pasture is the next of these zones. The chapter opens thus:

> On land unsuitable for farming, he should allot pastures for domestic animals (2.2.1),

which confirms the point that all other economic zones are designated only *after* land suitable for farming has been set aside. The text continues with the provision of wildernesses for Veda study by ascetics, forests for wild animals, forests for raw material and elephant forests. All these are secondary to designating land for farming and the settling of farmers on it. All these non-farming zones have different economic functions.

They also have different inhabitants. Farmlands are to be settled by farming families, mostly shudra farmers, in villages of one to five hundred families, grouped for administrative purposes into sets of 800, 400 and 200 villages. India is a country of small farms in which the family is the basic unit (even though there may be a landlord) and grows food for its own use, yielding a small surplus for the king and for acquiring necessities it cannot make for itself. This social and economic pattern relates to the farming villages, but outside that zone the conditions are quite different. The difference is observed in the description of the first duty of the overseer of pastures (vivita-adhyaksha):

> He should establish pasture land in regions between
> villages. He should clear lowlands and forests of the
> danger of robbers and wild animals.(2.34.6–7)

Pastures, then, are not simply taken as nature gives them, but are deliberately established and improved. If they lack water, the overseer of pastures is to sink wells or make other provision for the livestock to drink from. Pastures are established where farms and farming villages are not situated, including marshy lowlands and forests; and their inhabitants are not farming-families but robbers and wild animals. In other passages we hear of forest people, hunters and birdcatchers, who are not settled in their environment by the king like the farmers but are already there, and have a loose and ambiguous attachment to the kingdom. By contrast, the cowherd (gopa), as we have already seen, is given a plot in a farming village and does not reside in the pasture land where he carries out his activities, but with the farmers.

As to the two dangers to livestock, namely robbers and wild animals who inhabit the pasture zone, the robbers must have been the worse, and cattle-rustling must have been a constant occurrence, as the text gives considerable attention to its punishment, which was severe: death for killing an animal or inciting another to kill one, stealing or inciting another to steal (2.29.17). On the other hand, someone recovering cattle stolen by thieves is to be rewarded, and someone rustling cattle belonging to people of another country shall receive half the cattle as a reward, the rest going to the king, a transaction something like the sharing with the king the spoils of war.

Wild animals and forests are a matter of a different nature. Large carnivores, such as tigers and lions, require a considerable population of prey animals, such as the many kinds of deer, antelope and gazelle, which are the special richness of India's forests and wetlands. When cattle and other domestic animals are grazed in forests or grasslands they compete for the same forage, and in turn become prey for the meat-eaters.[1] It is here that the economy of the kingdom clashes with the natural ecology, and remoulds it for human benefit by clearing the forests where domestic animals are grazed. This certainly occurred in the time of the *Arthashastra*, and has become a sensitive issue today. Nowadays tigers must be protected against humans, not the other way around, through programmes such as Operation Tiger.

The different and more hard-to-control aspect of the human inhabitants of this zone add to the duties of the overseer of pastures that go beyond matters to do with grazing of animals. He must also monitor the problem of robbers and enemies through fowlers and hunters who patrol the forest and send warnings by sounding conch shells or drums. The overseer reports the movement of enemies and forest people to the king by messenger pigeons and through smoke signals.

Livestock that is herded includes cattle, buffaloes, horses, donkeys, camels, goats, sheep and pigs. Elephants are a special case as these are captured in the wild as adults. For all kinds of livestock the *Arthashastra*, following its pattern of model and variation, gives a detailed discussion of the two most important animals to the king, namely cattle and horses, and directs that herds of the other domestic species follow the same pattern.

Both the overseer of cattle (*go-adhyaksha*) and the overseer of horses (ashva-adhyaksha) are responsible for keeping track of the total number of animals in their charge and the different kinds and conditions of them. Herds of cattle owned by the king are given to herdsmen under two distinct kinds of contracts—wages and 'tending with a tax and a fixed return'. In the first case, a cowherd, buffalo herdsman, milkman, churner and hunter (to provide protection against robbers and wild animals) look after a herd of 100 milk cows for a wage, and the entire yield of the milk and ghee goes to the king. In the second case, one person is put in charge of a mixed herd of old cows, milk cows, cows with calves, pregnant cows and heifers, and is paid a share, eight *varakas* of ghee, one *pana* per animal and the hide of cattle that die, once a year. Perhaps such a person hires his own assistants to deal with such a large herd. Here, we have yet another enterprise in which the king and the worker are co-sharers.

Trade routes

Farmland and pasture land are the economic zones for the first two of the three branches of vartta, economics or the production of livelihoods. The third branch, which is trade, appears in these early chapters of Book Two not in the form of *marketplaces*, but of trade *routes*. Markets do appear later in the text, and we will be examining them in the next chapter. But I need to mention the somewhat unexpected fact that the *Arthashastra* discussion of economic topography connects trade with routes and not marketplaces. Here and elsewhere, a close reading of the *Arthashastra* gives one the sense that trade is thought of not in terms of *selling* in marketplaces but in terms of the *transportation* of goods from workplaces to buyers in markets, which differs greatly from the present-day market-centred methods of analysing trade. We shall see in the next chapter that the text has an underlying idea of the fair or true price of things sold in markets, which in the case of trade goods is proportional to their distance from the market. It also accords with the fact that workplaces are usually located near the source of raw materials, and have to be brought to market.

In its discussion of trade routes the *Arthashastra* speaks of land routes, water routes, and market towns (*panya-*

pattinam) (2.1.19). The roads are to be kept clear of harassments to traders by the king's favourites, works officers, robbers and frontier chiefs, or from being crowded by herds of cattle, so that trade is not hindered (2.1.38).

Mines

The *Arthashastra* considers mines to be the source of all wealth and power for the king:

> The treasury has its source in the mines; from the treasury the army comes into being; with the treasury and the army, the earth is obtained, with the treasury as its ornament. (2.12.37)

The overseer of mines (*akara-adhyaksha*), 'conversant with the science of metallic veins in the earth, metallurgy, smelting and the coloring of gems, or having assistants who are experts in these, and having skilled workers and tools', should examine old mines and new ones (12.1.1). Under his purview are the precious metals, gold and silver; the ordinary metals, bronze, copper, tin, vaikrintika, brass, steel, bell-metal, and iron; and gems. He has to not only actively manage the production of metals from ore, but also the workshops that produce the manufactured goods, and establish and oversee a trade in manufactured goods. The ordinary metals go to workshops established by an overseer of metals.

The overseer of the mint (*lakshana-adhyaksha*) supervises the minting of coins, which is a monopoly of the king, of silver and copper (but not gold coins during this period). Individuals can bring silver and copper to be turned into coins, but the charges are high, and only the king may make coins. The overseer of mines also establishes workshops for goods to be made from conch shells, diamonds, gems, pearls, corals and caustics, and sets up the trade in these. Salt is a royal monopoly administered by the salt commissioner, though it appears the manufacture of salt from seawater is done by individuals, and the duty of the overseer of salt (lavana-adhyaksha) is to collect the king's share, lease-rent and other royal dues, and to tax its sale. 'The buyers shall pay the duty and a protective duty corresponding to the loss sustained by the king's goods' (2.12.32). Brahmins learned in the Vedas, ascetics and labourers may take salt for their food (that is, for their own use but not for sale) without tax.

The king has a monopoly of subsoil deposits of metal ore and salt. The treatment of the duties of the overseer of mines gives a first impression that the production of these assets is also monopolized, but here and there the text makes it clear that the king also licensed others for a fee, or partnered with private entrepreneurs on a basis of shares in the profit, to work the mines and extract salt, similar to the co-sharing arrangements in other enterprises that we have already mentioned. Here the king-centred focus of the text may leave an exaggerated impression of the king's role, while in practice the role of private enterprise may have been greater. But there is no mistaking that metal ores and salt are considered specially important assets of the kingdom and that the king is closely involved in their extraction.

The taxing of salt is a royal privilege of great value. It touches the entire population of the kingdom without exception, since no one can live without salt. But the taxing of salt is, in our terms, very regressive, because the tax is a large proportion of the income of the poor, and a negligible proportion of the income of the rich, who eat no more salt than the poor. Indian kings regularly regarded salt as theirs to monopolize, license and tax. So did the British during their rule in India, and they took exceptional steps to prevent smuggling which always accompanies the taxing of salt, including an attempt to plant a continuous, impenetrable hedge around the borders of their territories.[2] Mahatma Gandhi opposed this unpopular and unfair tax with a Salt March to make illegal salt from seawater, provoking the British to jail him and the many who accompanied him.

Forests

There are three main kinds of royal forests: forests for wild animals (*mriga-vana*), forests for raw materials (*dravya-vana*) and elephant forests (*gaja-vana*) (2.2.5). While pasture land is for domestic animals (*pashu*), forests are for wild animals (*mriga*).

> He should cause an animal forest for the king's recreation to be laid out, one *goruta* in extent, with a single entrance, protected by a moat, containing shrubs and bushes bearing sweet fruits, having trees without thorns, with shallow pools of water and stocked with tame deer and other animals, containing wild animals with claws and fangs blunted, and having male and female elephants and cubs useful for hunting. (2.2.3)

In addition to this kind of pleasure-grove the king establishes other animal forests in which all wild animals are protected from hunting. We should probably infer from this that hunting was going on at a scale that caused animal numbers to decline, and that kings took steps to protect animals because of it.

The king is to establish forests for materials, one for each of the kinds of produce (*kupya*), and workshops for goods made from them, with forest people (*atavi*) attached to the forests.

> The Overseer of Kupya should cause forest produce
> to be brought in by guards in the materials forests;
> and he should start workshops for forest produce.
> And he should fix dues from those cutting materials
> forests, also penalties, except in cases of distress.
> (2.17.1–3)

Here the mention of distress suggests that the materials
forest is something like the granary, in serving as a
reserve from which to alleviate the distress of the people
at large in emergencies.

Finally, there is the elephant forest. The provisions
for these forests are given in considerable detail:

> On the border of the kingdom he should establish a
> forest for elephants guarded by forest people. The
> Overseer of the Elephant Forest (naga-vana-
> adhyaksha; evidently different from the Overseer of
> Elephants, gaja-adhyaksha, who supervises the
> elephant stables) should, with the help of guards of
> the elephant forest, protect the elephant forest
> whether on the mountain, along a river, along lakes
> or in marshy tracts, knowledgeable of its boundaries,
> entrances and exits. They should kill anyone slaying
> an elephant. A person bringing in a pair of tusks of an
> elephant dying naturally shall be given a reward of
> four and a quarter panas (2.2.6–9)

> Guards of elephant forests, aided by elephant
> keepers, foot-chainers, border guards, foresters and

attendants, their own scent masked by the urine and dung of elephants, their bodies covered with branches of the *bhallataki*, and moving with five or seven female elephant decoys, should ascertain the size of the herds of elephants, by means of signs provided by sleeping places, footprints, dung and damage cased to river banks. They should maintain a record in writing of every elephant, whether moving in a herd, moving alone, lost from a herd, leader of a herd, and whether wild, maddened, a cub, or released from captivity. (2.2.10–11)

This vivid picture has several features deserving mention: the active protection of elephants and harsh punishment of poachers, the keeping of an ongoing census of elephants in the forest, of different classifications and the use of forest people for the work. However, reverting to the description of the farmlands and villages at the beginning of this chapter, we find the elephant trainer and physician are settled there (along with the cowherd) by grant of the king. They are not forest people, and live in villages, but they supervise and direct forest people who live where they work.

Workshops

We have seen that the overseers of mines and forest produce are to start workshops to turn raw materials into goods, and establish trade in these goods, both regulating and participating in the trade. As to the workshops (karmanta), we are not given much detail about their organization and workings, except when it comes to the precious metals, in the chapter 'Overseer of Gold' (2.13).

The duty of the overseer of gold (suvarna-adhyaksha) is to construct a workshop for working of gold and silver into finished goods, and also to establish a goldsmith (sauvarnika) in the market highway to supervise artisans who receive gold and silver from individuals from the countryside and the city, to be worked into jewellery for them on piece-rate contracts. The two chapters on these officials give us somewhat of a close view at a workshop (2.13–14). The overseer of gold supervises a body of artisans 'doing the work of setting in gold', blowers, servants and dust-washers, who are to be thoroughly searched when they enter and leave, their tools and uncompleted work remaining in the workshop. Besides the sources of gold and silver, and the processes of removing impurities, the chapter devotes attention to the different kinds of ornamental work, which give added value to the object. The chapter on the goldsmith devotes its attention to work contracts and the fines imposed upon workshop artisans who fail to fulfil the bargain or sequester some of the precious metal they have been given by the customer. The matter of pilfering gold and silver is a common occupational hazard, and there is an extensive listing of ways in which artisans cheat customers. As there is always some loss of material in the process of manufacture, the text states the allowable amounts of loss so that artisans are not wrongly blamed.

Gold and silver play a large part both in the kingdom, as a store of wealth useful for the costly ventures of the state, including war and diplomacy, and also as signs of the king's pre-eminence. These precious metals are equally important to the people of the countryside and of the city as stores of wealth and as signs of status. There is nothing remarkable about this, as the same could be said about gold and silver in many countries. Gold and silver are useful measures of value and means of exchange internationally and it is because of this that gold and silver are highly valued in many countries. However, as we will see in the next chapter, India has a specially strong demand for gold and silver over a very long period of time, much more than other countries.

Another chapter of Book Two that invites us inside a workplace is the chapter on the duties of the overseer of textiles (*sutra-adhyaksha*, 2.23).

The Overseer of Textiles should cause trade to be carried out in thread, armour, cloth and rope through

persons expert in the work. He should get thread
spun out of wool, bark-fibre, cotton, silk-cotton,
hemp and flax, through widows, crippled women,
maidens, women who have left their homes and
women paying off their fine through personal labour,
through mothers of courtesans, through old female
slaves of the king and through female slaves of temples
whose service to the gods have ceased. (2.23.1–2)

There are several aspects about this passage that are very
interesting. At the outset it is apparent that manufacture
is divided by gender, women making thread and men
making the finished product. Secondly, the finished
product includes armour and rope, so an element of
military supply is involved. Thirdly, the women involved
in spinning are needy and lacking in protection or retired
from service, and hence providing work for them is a
way in which the king fulfils his duty to be the protector
of those who have no families or are otherwise
vulnerable. Protecting those who have none to look
after them is widely recognized to be a royal virtue.
Such women are not to be taken advantage of. Further
on in the chapter it says that those who remain at home
should be given work, through a female slave of the
overseer who meets them in their homes, or, if they are
able to come to the textile house, the overseer's man
should have an exchange of goods and wages at dawn,

under a lamp for the inspection of the thread, and if he looks her in the face or converses with her on any matter other than business he is to be fined (2.23.11–14).

The overseer of textiles gets cloth made by weavers with contracts stipulating the amount of work, time and wage—it appears to be a 'putting out' industry. But the text also speaks of workshops for weaving cloth (*sutrana-karmanta*) from fibres called *kshauma*, and *dukula*, from silk, hair of the *ranku* deer and cotton, for the production of varieties of cloth, bedsheets and coverings, and also starting workshops for armour (2.23.7–8).

Workers

Having examined the workplaces, we need to complete the picture by saying a word about the people who work in them.

Farming constitutes the norm for the *Arthashastra*. It is organized on the basis of the small family-farm producing food for its own consumption—the form that is called subsistence farming, as opposed to modern-day commercial farming in which the whole of the crop is sold for money. The subsistence farmer must exchange some of his crop for goods the family cannot make for itself, and must produce a surplus for paying taxes.

From the time of the *Arthashastra* to the recent past, India has been mainly a land of small-scale family-based farming. Large-scale plantation-farming occurred only to a limited degree (the king's own farmland, worked by serfs, wage labourers and those remitting fines would be an example), though large holdings by landlords was common. Nevertheless the *Arthashastra* mentions many forms of labour that depart from the norm of the free farmer and his family. These include slavery, forms of debt servitude and the wage-labour or share-cropping by people who do not own farmland.

The *Arthashastra* considers the enslavement of a person who is Arya by his kin a crime punishable by a severe fine, and this appears to apply to all four castes, brahmin, kshatriya, vaishya and shudra (3.13.1). At the same time, the whole discussion of this matter would be unnecessary if enslavement did not occur in fact, perhaps among all castes. Among *mlecchas* (non-Aryans, foreigners, barbarians), slavery is permitted as it is customary among them (3.13.3).

Debt-servitude appears frequently in the text, under several forms, as a voluntary servitude or temporary slavery during which working for a creditor pays off a debt. Further, we read more than once of persons remitting a fine or paying taxes through labour for the king on his farms or in mines or in workshops. Such temporary enslavement, as it can be termed, is cheap labour, but it is the least desirable form of labour for an employer, the worker being unskilled and temporary.

The existence of labour at a wage or on terms of share-cropping in the king's farms shows the presence of landless people in the countryside who must work for hire or for the use of farmland belonging to someone else. While debt and poverty drive many into temporary servitude, it is landlessness that creates the fundamental socio-economic division in the countryside, forcing the landless to work for the landowners on terms disadvantageous to themselves. While slavery has been abolished long ago in India, and indentured and bonded labour are very much things of the past, landless labour in the countryside continues to be a major presence, partly alleviated by the migration of the landless to cities in search of work.

One notices at many places in the *Arthashastra* that workers are frequently fined for substandard work by their employers, who seem to have the power to impose penalties at will. To illustrate this point, a good example would be those who take care of elephants:

> Uncleanliness of the stall, non-receipt of fodder,
> making elephants sleep on bare ground, striking them
> at an improper place, mounting by another person,
> riding at an improper time, or on unsuitable land,

leading down to water where there is no crossing, and taking them through a thicket of trees are reasons for penalty. The fine amount should be taken from their food and wages. (2.32.19–20)

However, at least as it concerns private individuals the king's judges will hear suits regarding disputes between employers and workers over wages, indicating the king's desire to find a balance between the interests of both classes. One gets an impression that while workers strike the best bargains they can get, there is a notion of customary rates of wages similar to the underlying notion we get of a just price for land and for the profits of the trader who brings goods to market, as we shall see in the next chapter.

In addition to unskilled or semi-skilled workers there is also the artisan class of people who possess skills of craftsmanship. This knowledge is their great asset and source of livelihood. Such workers may work on a piece-rate basis, receiving, say, gold from a customer to turn it into gold jewellery, or thread from the overseer of textiles to turn it into cloth, for an agreed price and in an agreed period of time, the artisan being responsible for the materials supplied to him and liable for an excessive diminution of the material during the process of manufacture. Or the artisan works at a wage in a workshop. There are some references to craft guilds of artisans who regulate prices and uphold standards among their members, showing that the artisans are more than workers at a wage, they are also owners of their tools and sellers of their work or of their finished goods, who enjoy, as a class, something of a collective monopoly of their kind of work, and therefore have some degree of control over the terms of their work. Merchants and traders are also organized into guilds and had a considerable amount of collective self-governing.

The economic landscape of the *Arthashastra*

Thus the landscape of the *Arthashastra* is divided into zones by the economy, and has a distinctive pattern. Farming comes first and everything else is assigned to land not taken up for farming. Farmers live in families, in villages. Others do, too. Cowherds, for example, are given land in villages; they do not live in the pastures where they do their work; pastures are inhabited by robbers and wild animals. Again, elephant-keepers and the physicians who care for them are given lands in villages—they do not live in elephant forests. On the other hand, forests contain forest people, who are very different from farmers, lying outside the caste system, organized in tribes. They are hard to control by the king but essential for the kingdom because they have valuable knowledge and skills pertaining to the forest that village-dwellers do not have. Troops for the army are recruited from forest people, but their loyalties are less certain for kings than other kinds of soldiers. They are especially useful as guides and scouts, fighting on certain kinds of terrain, countering certain modes of fighting, and fighting the enemy's forest troops (9.2.6–8). This is a little enigmatic, but we can draw an inference from it that forest troops have special knowledge and aptitudes that most soldiers do not, and that the king is wise to have them at his disposal. The *Arthashastra* does not give us much detail about the forest people, but it is evident that they are both an essential part of the royal enterprise because of their specialized knowledge of the forest zone, and one that is difficult to control because of it.

The farming-centred pattern of economic zones in the *Arthashastra* has a long history behind it, but it is not eternal. Pottery, woven cloth, metal-tipped ploughs and farming villages are the economic pattern that created Indian civilization long before the *Arthashastra*, but within measurable time. It is a pattern that emerged sometime after the ending of the last Ice Age 10,000 years ago, and it predates the rise of the earliest Indian cities in the Indus Valley nearly 5,000 years ago. It created a stability of life and a food-production surplus that allowed the creation of cities, kings and kingdoms, monumental architecture, luxury and fine arts patronized by kings and the aristocracies that supported them.

Scholars used to think that the great domestications that created this pattern belong to the Middle East—the domestication, that is, of wheat, barley, cattle, sheep and goats, all of which are found there in a wild state. It now appears, with the advance of archeological study of the Indus Civilization and the farming villages that preceded it, that all of these domestications of wild species may have occurred in India independently. The archaeologist Gregory Possehl proposes that India should be thought of as a part of the same, semi-arid ecological zone as the Middle East, in various parts of which the primary domestications occurred.[3] The domestication of rice, possibly in connection with early sites of rice domestication in South-east Asia, may also be an indigenous development. In any case, the economic pattern, and the shaping of the landscape into different economic zones in the *Arthashastra*, has ancient roots. It is the heart of the economy we find in the *Arthashastra*. And although it is ancient, it continues today. It is the basis upon which all subsequent economic development has been built.

5. MARKETS

HAVING EXAMINED THE inventory of desired goods in the *Arthashastra*, and the workplaces where they are made, we now need to look at markets where goods are exchanged. By using the term market we are not necessarily referring to *places* where transactions occur, but the transactions themselves, that is, *buying and selling*. I will limit the discussion to exchanges for a price denominated in money, leaving aside many sorts of barter or trade in kind.

We will see that private property and markets existed in the time of the *Arthashastra* but when we examine their working we will find many differences from the markets familiar to us today. We will see that the king is supposed to act to contain the extremes in price to protect merchants and the people in general. Underlying this policy is a feeling that goods have a proper price and that deviation from it is socially harmful. Merchants are valued for the positive social functions they perform by bringing goods to market, but the king has to be also alert about buyers being cheated.

The extent of markets

It is quite likely that in the time of Kautilya the bulk of the economic activity of the kingdom did not pass through markets, in the sense of buying and selling for money. It is apparent that the largest segment of the population were farmers, who provisioned themselves directly by raising crops and animals for their own consumption, and whose lands passed on to their sons as co-sharers, because of which the core activities did not involve markets. The king acted in the same way, but on a larger scale and with labourers working for him in the royal farmlands, mines, forests and workshops, provisioning the different elements of the kingdom, such as the royal family, the state employees and the army, directly and not through markets. Further, the main method in which a surplus was extracted from agriculture was through taxation, not through buying and selling.

But even subsistence farmers need markets for things they do not make for themselves, and city people who do not produce for themselves need markets even more. The king himself cannot do without trade and traders. Trade has a long history, and of the three branches of vartta, it is the oldest, preceding the invention of agriculture and the rearing of livestock by thousands of years, according to archaeologists. But farming villages need trade more than people who live by hunting and gathering, and kings and kingdoms especially need to procure supplies of common necessities and luxuries through trade. There is abundant evidence in texts and through archaeology that a vigorous trade and the use of coined money existed, including an international luxury trade which provided desirable signs of wealth and high status, at the time of the *Arthashastra*. Though the volume of money in circulation was small compared to our times, and the reach of the cash economy was much more modest, money was a significant part of the economy. The *Arthashastra* mentions the presence of markets at some length.

As with farming and herding, the king has a dual role in trade, being both a participant, making and selling royal goods, and a regulator (as well as a taxer) of the trade of the people. To a considerable extent the king provisioned the royal household directly, producing for its own needs through his servants. Insofar as he practised trade (through his officials, of course) one could call him an entrepreneur. But besides undertaking trade for profit to the royal household, he also had to regulate and tax the trade of others, keeping in view the health of the treasury and ensuring peace and good order among the people. As with farming, the king is both a player and a referee in markets and trading.

The most significant feature of the ancient economy for the practice and regulation of trade, and the one that makes it very different from economic conditions of today, is the comparative scarcity of capital and the very high degree of risk and uncertainty of the ancient economy, with sudden and dramatic changes of price. It will be necessary to keep this in mind as we examine the logic of the *Arthashastra*'s treatment of markets.

Property rights in land

Let us start with property rights in land. This is an extremely vexed question among historians because of the European doctrine of Oriental Despotism. According to this doctrine, in Asia the king was the owner of all the land, and everyone held land *of* the king, as a tenant, and the king could revoke the grant of land at his sweet will, any time. Is this model true? Does it apply to ancient India?

In ancient Greece, Aristotle had drawn a contrast

between the Greeks and the Persians which linked private property with political freedom among the Greeks, and the opposite among the Persians. He said that in Persia the Great King owned all the land, and hence all Persians were his slaves. In seventeenth-century Europe this doctrine was revived and applied to the Ottoman Empire. European political theorists such as Montesquieu linked European freedom to strong property rights in land, while associating Oriental Despotism to royal ownership of all land under the Ottoman Turkish caliphs. Once the British East India Company acquired territorial rule in Bengal and needed an overall conception of Indian rights in land, some British writers extended this doctrine to the Mughals but not to the ancient kingdoms. Others extended it to the ancient kingdoms as well, while still others argued against it. The British differed among themselves whether Oriental Despotism properly described the Indian kingdom, but it became the prevailing view. The Oriental Despotism thesis provided a rationale for giving British rulers of India broader powers than were allowed in Britain itself, under the concept of a division of executive, judicial and legislative powers. For example, the British collector of a district in India was given both executive and judicial powers. The British justified the use of powers considered despotic by saying these were customary in India and were used to prepare India for a transition from despotism to a liberal government.[1]

The policy question was rooted in an interpretation of ancient Indian history that held there was no private property because the king owned all the land. The question has been much debated by historians. Lallanji Gopal has assembled very convincing evidence against the Oriental Despotism interpretation of ancient Indian kingship in a classic article.[2] Having property in land means having powers to enjoy it, namely the power to use, sell, lease, mortgage, give or bequeath, unhindered by others. The king, to be sure, had wide-ranging powers, but by and large in ancient times the king and the landowner were considered to have concurrent rights of different kinds, the king's being the right to tax the land. The king's tax was often called a share (bhaga), implying that the king and the farmer were both entitled to a share of the harvest. In other words, they were co-sharers. We have seen in this book that there were many enterprises in which the king featured as a co-sharer along with private individuals, in a relation of partnership. The land tax, which implies the taxation of the farmer's crop, was the foremost enterprise in which the concept of sharing was applied.

With these considerations in mind, let us see what the Arthashastra has to say about the sale of land, which of course is a leading sign of private property, since to sell property, one must be an owner. Here is the relevant passage:

> Kinsmen, neighbours and creditors, in that order, shall have the right to buy land that is for sale. After that, others who are outsiders may buy. Owners shall proclaim a dwelling for sale in front of the house, in the presence of members of forty neighbouring families, and a field, a park, an embankment, a tank or a reservoir at the boundaries, in the presence of village elders who are neighbours, according to the extent of the boundary, saying, 'At this price who is willing to buy?' When it has been proclaimed three times without objection, the buyer is entitled to buy. But, if the price increases because of competition among the buyers, the excess together with the tax shall go to the treasury. The buyer at the sale shall pay the tax. (3.9.1–6)

There is no question that the passage shows the power to sell, which implies private ownership of land in the ordinary sense.

But that is not the end of the matter, because the passage also gives us several details that depart from what we may expect in a present-day real-estate transaction. Since we are familiar with free, price-making markets we are liable to take this evidence of private property also to be evidence of free markets. But private property is not necessarily the same thing as a free market. In the free-market model, buyers and sellers are free to offer whatever prices they wish, and the price at which supply and demand are in balance will clear the market, finding a buyer for every unit of a good offered for sale. If there is an abundance of eager buyers and a dearth of sellers, the buyers will bid up the price in competition with one another. If there is an abundance of sellers and fewer buyers, the reverse will happen and prices will fall. Prices move up or down until a price is found that balances out the available supply and the effective demand.

There are several ways in which the sale of land in the *Arthashastra* deviates from this model. In the first place priority is given to a kinsman, neighbour and creditor over the stranger. This manner of ranking gives the buyers unequal priority in the sale and removes the transaction from the free-market model. In particular, it recognizes the strong connection of farmland with the family among farmers in ancient India, since a kinsman as the buyer is privileged over all other buyers. In the second place, the *Arthashastra* insists that the transaction be transparent, being conducted in the presence of knowledgeable witnesses, that is, neighbours—as many as forty of them—and that the price be announced, not once but three times, 'without objection'. What objection? Most assuredly an objection from a witness would be about the commonly accepted value, and therefore the proper price, of the land. Here and elsewhere the *Arthashastra* opposes and even punishes deals made in secrecy as the very antithesis of its ideal for markets. It is because transactions hidden from public view can deviate from the true price. Thirdly, the underlying logic in the passage is the belief that there is a proper, customary price that reflects the true value of the land. It is the just price, not a market price reached by the free interaction of the forces of supply and demand. That is what the *Arthashastra* aims to achieve. Among farming societies in recent times, the customary price of land is related to the annual yield of the land, such as ten times the annual yield; perhaps something like that is the practice on which this passage relies. Finally, the king not only levies a tax on the transaction— no surprise there—but he also confiscates the excess amount if bidding among buyers pushes the price above the true value.

In short, the king acts to limit or even suppress fluctuations in prices resulting from the interplay of supply and demand factors. In practice, if there is an announced price at a rate which all agree to be proper and customary, and there are multiple buyers, and if the king sequestered any excess of price caused by a competition among buyers, the sale would fall to the buyer solely on the criterion of social nearness to the seller. This is very different from the price-making markets we are familiar with today.

The conclusion we must draw from this analysis is that there *is* true private property in the hypothetical kingdom of the *Arthashastra*. But it is conditioned by the prior claims of kinship, neighbourhood, indebtedness and other conditions, and it is biased against strangers. Moreover it differs from the modern ideal of a free market. The king acts to *prevent* the formation of a price-making market in land with freely fluctuating prices, in favour of enforcing a price reflecting the current perception of true values by those who are in a position to know—the neighbouring farmers.

The sale of goods

We find a similar logic at work in a different setting, outside the city gates where merchandise arrives and is subject to inspection by the overseer of customs (*shulka-adhyaksha*). The levying of taxes on transactions is one of the leading objects of royal surveillance, but besides contributing to the treasury, Kautilya wants the king to restrict wide-scale fluctuations in prices.

In order to understand this transaction, we need to know that in the time of the *Arthashastra* it was often the practice to separate long-distance trade from local trade, each being conducted by different bodies of traders. The place the two meet is at the city gate. Long-distance traders brought goods in bulk to the gate, where they were bought by local traders to sell at retail inside the city. Long-distance traders were not allowed to sell at retail.[3] The city gate is the location where the wholesalers and the retailers meet and transact business. It is also the place where the king imposes taxes in the form of customs duties.

> Traders shall declare the quantity and price of the goods that have arrived at the foot of the flag before the city gate. 'Who is willing to purchase these goods, so much in quantity, at this price?'—when it has been proclaimed three times, he should give it to those who have sought it. If there is competition among buyers, the increase in price together with the duty shall go to the treasury. If the trader declares the quantity of the goods or the price to be less than it actually is, so as to lower the duty, the king shall confiscate the difference, or the trader shall pay eight times the duty . . . If the trader increases the price beyond the proper price of that commodity to stave off a rival buyer, the king shall receive the increase in

price or impose double the amount of duty (2.21.7–
11, 13).

Here we see the same motives at play. The intent to
conduct market exchanges in conditions of full publicity;
the intent to ensure that goods sell for a proper price
reflecting their true value; the intent to confiscate an
excess of the true value caused by competitive bidding
among buyers; in short, to contain fluctuations in price
due to changes in the supply–demand relation.
Furthermore, the king's official is to implement steps to
punish traders (and in the process enrich the treasury)
for trying to evade the proper price by fraud. The
punishments are severe.

These principles apply generally, both in the country
and at the city gate. But unlike the sale of land in the
village, where villagers who know the customary value
of land are present as expert witnesses, at the city gate
there are no such expert witnesses. Here that function
belongs to the overseer of trade (*panya-adhyaksha*).
Consequently, knowledge of prices figures largely in
the duties of this overseer, as we see in the following job
description:

> The Overseer of Trade should be conversant with
> the differences in the prices of goods of high value
> and of low value, and the desirability or undesirability

of goods of various kinds, whether produced on land
or in water and whether they have arrived by land
routes or water routes, and he should know about
times when it is appropriate to disperse or concentrate
markets, and for buying or selling. (2.16.1)

In the passage, the matter of dispersing or concentrating
markets may seem obscure, but as we follow the text we
see that it has to do with containing extreme fluctuations
of prices. If there is surfeit of some commodity which
leads to a price drop, the overseer of trade is to
concentrate goods in one place by establishing a single
marketplace for it and raise the price, so as not to ruin
the traders who are the sellers (2. 16.2–3). In the reverse
situation:

If there is a glut of certain commodities, the Overseer
of Trade should sell all goods in one place. So long as
they remain unsold, others are forbidden to sell such
goods. The agents shall sell them for a daily wage for
the benefit of the subjects (i.e. at a moderate price)
(4.2.33–35).

Here the overseer of trade intervenes and has his agents
sell the commodity whose price he is trying to raise so
as not to ruin the sellers. At the same time he is to avoid
excess profit-taking, even on royal goods, so as not to
create a hardship for buyers who are the general public,
as we shall see in this passage:

He should establish in one place, trade in royal goods that are produced in his own country, in many places, those produced in foreign lands. And he should cause both to be sold so as to favour the subjects (i.e. at a reasonably low price). And he should avoid even a big profit that would be injurious to the subjects. He should not create a restriction as to time or the evil of a glut in the market in the case of perishable goods (2.16.4–7).

The notion of fair profit is implied in the advice that the overseer of trade should fix a profit for traders of five per cent above the permitted purchase price of local goods, and ten per cent for foreign goods. This links profit with the cost of bringing things to the market, by making it proportionate to the distance, virtually a charge for transportation. The objective of the policy is to keep traders in business by assuring them a fair profit and protecting them from a fall in prices due to a glut of goods, but also to keep prices and profits from rising excessively, and harming consumers. The idea is that private business enterprise is valuable to society and to the king, by bringing distant goods to buyers, but that its search for profit needs to be kept proportional to the benefit it delivers, and the people should be able to get goods at reasonable and stable prices.

Throughout, the aim is to strike a balance among the

king's profit, the merchant's profit and the public's need for a supply of goods at a fair and steady price. The goal, in a word, is to buffer the supply–demand forces or at least the extreme swings of price that follow from them. The *Arthashastra* shows an understanding of supply–demand forces, but treats them as a problem to be solved, or contained within tolerable limits, by royal action. Again, severe penalties are the means for attaining the goal: 'For those who increase the price beyond that or secure a higher profit during purchase or sale, the fine shall be two hundreds panas for an excess of five percent, and the same for an increase in price' (4.2.28–30). The severity of the penalties surely indicates the inability of the king's men to enforce the policy in practice.

In the case of the sale of land the fair price is determined by farmers themselves, who are considered the experts, but for other market transactions, there is no equivalent body of similar knowledge. The *Arthashastra* puts price setting in the hands of the overseer of trade, and relies on his expertise to determine the right value:

> In the case of commodities distant in place and time, the Overseer of Trade, expert in determining prices, shall fix the price after calculating the investment, the production of goods, duty, interest, rent and other expenses. (4.2.36)

This requires wide knowledge and skill, but of course in the hands of a single official it is inevitably somewhat arbitrary and subject to abuse.

Accustomed as we are to price-making markets, it is easy for us to see the downside of this policy—difficulty and costs of enforcing a fair-price market; the invitation it gives to various kinds of evasion such as smuggling and black-market transactions; the flatness of incentives under such a system, turning the energies of merchants toward adulteration and false declarations as means of increasing returns. Instead of asking whether such a system could actually work, however, we should ask why the author of the *Arthashastra* found it attractive. What was the logic in the conditions prevailing at that time? I suggest that, in the present day, even though we believe in free markets, when prices rise or fall steeply in an economic crisis, we exert pressure upon the government to intervene and save us from the consequences of price-making markets. For price-making markets are *good* only in the sense that they are *efficient*. The market price clears the market; but it may also be an extreme price that bankrupts sellers or starves buyers even while it works efficiently, as it should, according to its own nature. If steep price-changes provoke us to demand government protection from the price-making free market in our day and age, it is likely that extreme fluctuations of price and uncertainty about future prices were even greater in the times of the *Arthashastra*, and therefore posed greater danger to the king and his people, than the dampening effect of policies that tried, no doubt very imperfectly in practice, to maintain a regime of uniform and expected prices.

Foreign trade

The *Arthashastra* favours foreign trade, and urges the king to take part in it through his overseer of trade.

> He should encourage the import of goods produced in foreign lands by allowing concessions. And to those who bring such goods in ships or caravans, he should grant exemptions from taxes that would enable them to make a profit. And no lawsuit in money matters should be allowed against foreign traders, except such as are members of local guilds and their associates. (2.16.11–13)

Thus the import of goods is treated as a desirable practice, entirely to be encouraged. But while the import of goods is considered advantageous, exporting to foreign lands should be permitted only for those goods that are in abundant supply within the kingdom. This thinking is oriented toward the goods rather than money profits. It appears to be contrary to current views, which wants exports to exceed imports, so that the trade balance is favourable to one's own country. The overseer of trade is to undertake trade with foreign countries on behalf of the king and for a profit. It is presumed to be a land trade, and part of the overseer's work is to be in contact with leaders of the countryside, the forest and the frontier to assure a safe journey for the caravan of goods.

Returning to a point made in the opening pages about the comparison of northern and southern trade routes, and the advantage of the latter, we are now in a position to appreciate its entire meaning. Here is the passage in full:

'The route to the Himalaya is preferable to the southern route (Dakshinapatha), for the commodities of elephants, horses, perfumes, ivory, skins, silver and gold are of very high value,' say the teachers. No, says Kautilya. These with the exception of blankets, skins and horses, and with the addition of conch shells, diamonds, rubies, pearls and gold are more plentiful on the southern route. (7.12.22–24)

All the items in this comparative list of goods are precious goods or the strategic goods, horses and elephants. In spite of the great importance of ordinary metals and other items of kupya for the success of the army and the economy in general, the value of long-distance trade rests in treasure and the two animals upon which depend the fortunes of war.

We have seen in the inventory of goods named in the *Arthashastra* (chapter three) that the implied horizon of trade reached from the China-silk of East Asia to the horses of Central Asia and Vanayu (Iran or Arabia), to the red coral of the Roman Mediterranean. Virtually the whole of Eurasia participated in a long-distance trade in luxuries.

The framework of law

Market exchanges need a framework of law to operate effectively, the law providing a peaceful method to resolve disputes among parties to a transaction, on the one hand, and, on the other, meting out punishment for improper behaviour in the market. The *Arthashastra* devotes two books, Book Three and Book Four, to two types of courts with two kinds of judges administering two kinds of law. We need to examine them, and see how markets enter in.[4]

The first kind of law is called the Law of Transactions (*vyavahara*), and it concerns disputes between two parties, mostly of a contractual nature. Such disputes are heard and acted upon by a panel of three judges (*dharmastha*) appointed by the king, having the rank of ministers.

Such judges are to be available at the major administrative nodes of the kingdom: the frontier post, the headquarters of ten villages, the headquarters of 400 villages, and the capital city. These cases are in the nature of civil suits, in which an aggrieved party takes the initiative by bringing a suit and seeking a judgment against the defendant. Doubtless there were other means of third-party resolution of disputes outside of such courts. The overseer of trade himself is to be an arbitrator in disputes between foreign and indigenous traders (which is to say the long-distance traders dealing in bulk and the local retailers) and other sources speak of merchant guilds that resolved disputes among their members. But beyond that, the entirety of Book Three is devoted to the adjudication by the king's judges of disputes arising from 'transactions'.

This is a very important part of the *Arthashastra*. It has every appearance of being based on real courts, and the real-world process of devising rules for settling disputes that cannot be settled by the parties and are brought to the king for judgment. Transactions are divided into categories, and most of them we would consider contracts of some kind. This is the list:

Marriage, inheritance, immovable property, non-observance of conventions, debt, deposits, slaves and workers, partnership, sale and purchase, gifts, sale without ownership, robbery, slander, battery, gambling and betting, miscellaneous.

Disputes arising from all such transactions are in the nature of civil suits or civil wrongs (what lawyers call torts) in that they come before the king's judges only if a complaint is brought by the aggrieved party. They allow for the peaceful settlement of disputes and the keeping of the peace and are essential for the functioning of markets. Of course they do so at a price, namely the fines and court costs imposed on the losing party by the king's judges.

It is reasonably certain that this real law was first formulated in writing in the arthashastra tradition, and only later absorbed into the dharmashastra tradition, beginning with the Laws of Manu. In Manu and later texts we find a section on the eighteen 'feet' of transactions (vyavahara) or dispute (*vivada*), contained within a new topic of Rajadharma, which does not exist in earlier dharma texts. It is entirely possible that the *Arthashastra* of Kautilya was the source of this material on transactions for the Laws of Manu.[5]

While Book Three of the *Arthashastra* is devoted to civil suits or civil wrongs, including the economic relations of employer and employee, partnerships, sellers and buyers and so forth, the very next part, Book Four, is something akin to our criminal law, in which the king, rather than the aggrieved party, takes the initiative and sets the judicial process in motion, rather than adjudicating disputes that happen to be brought before him by his subjects. The king takes the initiative to punish crimes because they are felt to be wrongs against the kingdom at large. This concept has the colourful name of the 'removal of thorns'. The thorns are the miscreants whom the king punishes. These courts consist of panels of three magistrates (pradeshtri), having the rank of ministers, to whom the king delegates his powers in this department, in other words, an entirely separate cadre of judges which is separate from the previously described courts for disputes arising from transactions.

Artisans (*karukara*) and traders (*vaidehaka*) figure among the thorns and the king watches over them, punishing them when they stray. In fact, the first two topics of Book Four are called 'Keeping a Watch over Artisans' and 'Keeping a Watch over Traders'. Under artisans we hear of weavers, washermen, tailors, goldsmiths and workers of other metals, physicians and actors. The text speaks of all the problems associated with artisans, including shortage in measure, absconding with material entrusted to them to be worked upon, non-performance of contracted work, counterfeiting and similar offences. With respect to traders the problems that arise include inaccurate weights and measures, counterfeit goods, collusion over prices and earning excessive profit. It is under the rubric of 'removal of thorns' that the king is to pursue the containment of the profiteering of traders, by means of harsh punishment:

> For artisans and artisans who by conspiring together bring about deterioration in the quality of work or increase in profit or cause a hindrance to buying or selling, the fine is one thousand panas. For traders, too, who by conspiring together to hoard goods (to create an artificial scarcity in order to raise prices) or sell them at a high price, the fine is one thousand panas. (4.2.18–19)

A penalty of a thousand panas is ruinously high, and one imagines few would be able to pay such fines and would have to resort to debt-servitude by working for the king to pay it off—a very heavy punishment. The severity of the penalties attests that price fluctuations could be contained only partly and with difficulty, that surveillance of the market was never complete, so that strong measures had to be in place. Harsh measures would instill a sense of fear that in the unlikely event of being caught one would pay dearly.

Overall, the attitude of the king toward trade and commerce was favourable but mixed, compared with the unalloyed enthusiasm for increasing the extent of farmed land and farmers. Trade is to be enhanced, to be sure, creating trade routes and making them safe; traders and the general public are to be protected from wide fluctuations in prices; import of goods from foreign countries is to be encouraged by allowing a higher profit, though the drain of goods to foreign countries is to be discouraged; the king is to be a trader himself and profit by it. But manipulation by artisans and traders in conducting their business had to be detected and punished for the good of the whole. There is no comparable suspicion of farmers in the way they worked. From the king-centred view, farming is the great creator of wealth, and not commerce.

This comes as a surprise, given that, as we have seen, kingship requires for its working a continuing supply of luxuries, all of them costly, many of them from distant places, both to maintain the magnificence of the court and to supply the army with horses. One might expect the economics of kingship to be better attuned to the wealth-making potential of the commercial and trading sector for that reason. Even when kings came to depend upon private bankers to finance their wars they remain oriented toward farming and the land. Commerce and trade came to the forefront of the economic order much later in history, bringing the middle class to the forefront of the political order.

6. CONCLUSION

THE *ARTHASHASTRA* IN THE LONG VIEW

THE *ARTHASHASTRA* GIVES us a king-centred perspective on wealth and power. In it we see a concern for provisioning the royal household and army, and of alleviating famine in the kingdom, through the building and stocking of storehouses of different kinds. Its way of evaluating goods puts the emphasis upon treasure for warfare, foreign relations and for making visible the king's pre-eminence through the display of luxury. The organization of the kingdom into different economic zones gives first place to farming and the farming village. Its market policies try to sustain ideals of fair price and contain extreme fluctuations of price. It has two kinds of courts that provide for the peaceful settlement of disputes over transactions and the 'removal of thorns' from the kingdom.

We have seen that, in its time, kingship and the sangha or republic are the main political forms. The great advantage of the republic is the solidarity of its governing class, each member having a strong sense of responsibility for the whole. This makes the republic a formidable enemy and a desirable ally, and it could only be defeated by destroying the strong fellow-feeling of its members through 'sowing dissent'. Kingship, by unifying power in a single royal family is less cohesive and vulnerable to overthrow by assassination or army coup. But its economic advantage over republics is superior and outweighs the disadvantages. In the long run kingdoms prevailed over republics.

The long reign of kingship

The main advantage of kingship over a republic is economic. It rests on a greater ability to amass capital. The king is able to tax the three branches of vartta or production of livelihood—farming, rearing of livestock and trading. The king also participates in these branches through his agents, a kind of householding on a grand scale, and regulates them as well. However, it requires employing people with expert knowledge, the very knowledge that the *Arthashastra* captures for us in Book Two, which is both a rare and a very hard record to decipher because of its expert nature. The king maintains public order by resolving disputes and imposing fines and court costs, which also adds to the treasury. In so doing he creates an internal *peace*. The king licenses the working of mines and the production of salt, another source of royal income. The king has the right to impose additional taxes in an emergency, and can use hidden means to replenish a depleted treasury. At every step, then, the *Arthashastra* shows that the success of the king rests on a robust economy, in which he participates through undertaking economic enterprises, through regulation and fines, and above all through taxation.

At every step we meet, not the idea of despotism and the royal ownership of everything, but the idea of the king's share (bhaga). We meet, not Aristotle's tendentious assessment of the constitution of the Persian Empire, according to which the king owned all and everyone was his slave, but a more entrepreneurial concept according to which the king is a co-sharer with the people of the kingdom in various wealth-making enterprises, resorting to language drawn from fathers and sons working their agricultural land together or partnership of traders and merchants. The focus is not on ownership of a resource but of a share of what is produced. The co-sharers are by no means equal, but there is at the heart of the idea of the share a certain sense of mutual interest among co-sharers to promote production, as then all shares will be larger. This concept seems to motivate, for example, the advice that the king should take away land that the farmer does not cultivate and give it to someone who will.

The formidable powers of the king to amass wealth are also powers to advance the general prosperity of the kingdom by prudent policies of extending farming, herding and trading, or to lessen profiteering by the imposition of punitive taxes and fines. There is no magic formula by which the king can ensure his success and avoid catastrophe. Everything depends upon his finding a proper balance among overlapping and sometimes competing ends: a full treasury, a strong army, a prosperous people and effective means of resolving disputes to maintain the peace of the kingdom. The *Arthashastra* cannot guarantee success but it shows kings and their ministers the way to a rational approach in making choices. Finally, the notion of the king having a share in the productive enterprises of his people promotes a kind of enlightened self-interest, and not the unlimited extraction of wealth and resources. Finding the balance is the aim of the *Arthashastra*.

How well was this balance kept in actual ancient

kingdoms? It is impossible to know directly, and every case is unique. But we have indirect evidence of the success of kings, of royal families and of kingship itself in the tenure of their reign. While the ancient period, as seen through the record of inscriptions, gives us a picture of more or less constant warfare over the control of farming populations and other assets, and of succession disputes within the royal family, this picture of endless change occurs within a largely stable political and economic structure. And the wars of succession and territorial expansion seem not to have been too disastrous for the kings who undertook them.

In the late classical period, following the gradual dissolution of the Gupta Empire in about 550 CE till the establishment of the Turkish Sultanate of Delhi shortly after 1200 CE, we find a pattern of more or less durable regional centres governed by dynasties that were very long-lasting. To be sure, the regional powers were engaged in warfare with their rivals contesting control of intervening regions, but the kingdoms themselves endured for centuries. The average length of reign for kings of this period was a long twenty years, giving substantial political stability. As the average length of a king's reign (twenty years) was not much less than the average length of generation (twenty-five years), it is evident that succession disputes were not so frequent as to upset the stability of rule. Many royal dynasties ruled for hundreds of years. Among the longest are the Eastern Chalukyas, a buffer state in the Deccan, which lasted 400 years. The reign of the Palas of Bengal and the Cholas of the south endured for over 300 years, which gave a great deal of political stability amid changing kings and constantly shifting boundaries between kingdoms.[1] We can infer from this political stability that the economic policies that financed the kingdoms making up this interstate structure must have been effective on the whole.

It is the technical detail of the *Arthashastra*'s economic prescriptions that give us some insight into the economic underpinnings of the long reign of kingship, which has only recently come to an end. On the other hand, the *Arthashastra* does not tell us everything we might like to know about the ancient economy. There are some aspects of the economy that are obscure or even invisible in the *Arthashastra*, because they are thrown into the shadows by its king-centred point of view. Let us consider a few examples of the aspects of the economy that the *Arthashastra*, from its particular angle of view, does *not* illuminate so well, but which we can learn about from other ancient sources.

In the *Arthashastra*, we read a fair amount about working people and artisans (as discussed in chapter five) for which we are grateful because ancient literary works are mainly written by and for elites and do not often give us a true picture of the lives of people in the lower echelons of society. We learn about artisans of various kinds, under the rubric of keeping watch over their misbehaviour, such as weavers, washermen, tailors, goldsmiths and other metalworkers. But the potter is practically invisible in the *Arthashastra* simply because of the low valuation of pottery in the text, and the evident absence of luxury pottery at the time, even though the potter's works were a necessity for everyone and a virtually indestructible product of the ancient economy that archaeology relies upon to construct its chronologies. Indeed archaeology is one of the best means we have to learn new things about the ancient economy and the lives of ordinary people that we cannot get by consulting Sanskrit texts.[2]

Traders and merchants are visible in the *Arthashastra*, but are somewhat in the background and appear as persons to be regulated, taxed and kept under watch for sharp practices. The measures adopted by the overseer of trade to correct a crash in prices due to a glut imply recognition of the social value of the trader's work, but the overall attitude is that traders' tendencies are to cheat customers and take profits in ways the author deems to be antisocial.

What the *Arthashastra* does not show us is the way in which the widening circulation of trade and money served to create a new phenomenon, the rich merchant, whose wealth began to rival that of the king. The Buddhists celebrated such a merchant, Anathapindaka, because he used his vast wealth to support the religion. What is intriguing about the stories of Anathapindaka is the confrontation between the rich merchant and the king in a sort of contest of wealth. Anathapindaka wished to purchase a wooded tract of land from prince Jeta, called the Jetavana, as a gift for the order of monks, a place for their rainy season retreat. The prince, who did not want to sell, named what he thought was an impossible price—as many coins as would cover the ground of the Jetavana. Images of Anathapindaka on Buddhist monuments such as the sculptures at Barhut in Madhya Pradesh, now in the National Museum in Kolkata, show Anathapindaka bringing bags of coins by ox cart and laying the rectangular coins of the time on the ground, like tiles on a floor, as the purchase price.[3] The story celebrates the piety of the merchant, but it also signals for us the possibility of private citizens possessing large fortunes, rivalling the wealth of the king.

The wealth of the rich merchant, then, might exceed that of the king. Generation of wealth by merchants did not arise independent of the king, but on the contrary, it arose through interactions of merchants with kings, especially through the luxury trade. As we have seen, the post-Mauryan age is the age of an acceleration in trade between Rome and India, to which the *Arthashastra* attests by mentioning the sources of certain luxury goods, without stating it explicitly. (The *Arthashastra*'s preference for the value of the southern route over the northern route is an additional testimony to the importance of this trade.) We have three very good sources of further information about the trade: a Greek sailor's manual about the trade between Roman Egypt, Africa, Arabia and India (the *Periplus of the Erythraean Sea*); reference to Greek traders in classical Tamil poetry (the Sangam literature); and an archaeological site in Tamil Nadu (Arikamedu). While the *Arthashastra* is oriented to the interior of north India, these sources give us a clearer window on long-distance trade through their orientation toward the coast of the Indian peninsula.

E.H. Warmington, examining this trade on the basis of the Roman author Pliny, the *Periplus* and the Tamil sources, concluded that the trade between Rome and India was more favourable to India, and caused a severe drain of Roman gold and silver coins to India.

Not only did Italy consume more than she produced, not only was Rome a city and Latium a district poor in manufactures, so that neither is mentioned in the lists of exports in the Periplus, but the [Roman] Empire taken as one unit was often unable to offer to foreign regions in general and to oriental nations in particular sufficient products of its own to balance the articles imported from them in large quantities, and the result of this was the draining away from the Empire of precious metals in the form of coined money without any adequate return.

A large proportion of this drain of gold and silver coin went to south India and the east and west coasts of the Deccan, as indicated by the find-spots of many buried hoards of Roman coins.[4] Gold shows up frequently in the Tamil poems of the Sangam literature.

The Tamil poems call Greeks engaged in the Roman trade with India *yavanar* (Ionians), mentioning them in contexts of luxury, trade, royalty, and royal gift-giving. Here is one such passage, in a poem by Nakkiranar praising the Pandya king Maran, likening him to the gods, in the translation of George Hart and Hank Heifetz:[5]

. . . May you live on, with a sweet life,
giving away precious ornaments to all those who
come to you in need
and never running out of them, while every day you
take your pleasure as women

wearing their shining bangles bring you the cool and
fragrant wine
carried here in their excellent ships by the Greeks
and the women pour it
for you out of pitchers made of gold that have been
fashioned with high
artistry, O Maran, you whose sword is raised on
high, like the sun
with its rays of heat driving away the darkness that
has filled in
the spaces of the beautiful sky, like the moon that
spreads
out its cool rays in the west, may you live
long and as firmly established as they are together
with the world!

The poem paints a word picture of the king, or rather
two word pictures. In the first, he is at leisure in the
palace, and in the second, his sword is raised to signify
war. In the first, wine is spoken of, and Greek ships are
mentioned to signify the richness and rarity of the wine,
that it comes from the faraway Mediterranean. Martha
Selby, a leading scholar of the Sangam poetry, observes
that Greeks figure in this poem as also in others, 'as a
matter of fact, as a part of royal material culture',
remarkable for being normal.[6]

We see here how luxury is portrayed to display the

king's greatness by his consumption of expensive and exotic products such as wine from the Mediterranean, in a vessel whose richness and rarity is conveyed by it being made of gold and poured by richly adorned serving women. The overall theme of the passage is the king's practice of giving precious ornaments to those who come to him in distress—including, in all probability, the poet. Luxury is turned into the royal virtue of liberality by gifting it away. Royal magnificence and royal gift-giving is the subject of many poems of the Sangam anthologies. The Roman trade in luxuries coincided with this efflorescence of courtly poetry, and the early days of kingship in the Tamil country when the 'three crowned kings' of the south, Chola, Pandya and Chera, were forming alliances with lesser chiefs and supporting new court poetry through their gifts of luxury goods. Kingship, poetry and the foreign trade in luxuries grew together and fed one another.

Archaeological excavations at Arikamedu, near Pondichery in Tamil Nadu, further confirm this picture. Arikamedu was the site of a trading station of the Indo-Roman trade, which is to say, a warehouse for the storage of goods arriving from the Mediterranean and a collection-point for Indian goods to be exported. Among the finds were Roman wine-vessels, called amphoras, and other ceramics of a kind called Arretine, shipped from Italy, giving material evidence of the trade which brought Italian wine in Greek ships to the Pandya king. The amphoras date to the first century BCE. Accompanying the site report is an inventory of hoards of Roman coins from India and Sri Lanka, numbering eighty different finds, some of them large. Roman coinage is found at many find-spots along the coast of the peninsula, and further inland near sites of ancient gemstone mining. It seems this coinage circulated in Indian markets. Later Roman emperors debased the coins, that is, they adulterated them with cheaper metals. When the standard of Roman gold coinage was debased, Indian kings such as the Guptas began issuing gold coins from their own mints.[7]

This account could be greatly lengthened. Enough has been said, however, to make the point that the *Arthashastra* shows quite clearly the association of the economy of ancient India with kingship, but it does not tell us everything we may wish to know about this relationship, and to fill in some of the details we need to resort to other surviving texts, to archaeological excavations and even to poetry to shed light on what the *Arthashastra* leaves obscure.

Kings, royal families and kingship itself have been very successful in India, as judged by their long duration, and superior in wealth and power to the ancient republic.

Kingship is the old regime which has been replaced by the modern republic. We need now to ask why kingship, so successful for such a long time, is fading away and how the transition came about.

The long view

How does the picture of the ancient economy relate to the present day? What changes have occurred from the ancient system of the relationship between kingship and the economy that we read of in the *Arthashastra* and in other sources? If kingship was so successful then, why is it dying now? It will help us track the changes if we separate them into political and economic ones for purposes of analysis (although, as the *Arthashastra* teaches, they are intimately connected in fact), and then bring them together to examine their interaction in the present. This will give us a picture of the long view that joins the time of the *Arthashastra* with our own time space by means of the transformations that have come between.

To take the political side first, the long reign of kingship intervenes between the ancient republics, discussed in Book Eleven of the *Arthashastra*, and the republic of India.

The republic was reinvented in modern times by the American Revolution (1776) and the French Revolution

(1789). Their leaders invoked the history of the ancient Roman Republic and the democracy of Athens as models, and the framers of the Indian constitution, likewise, invoked the history of the sanghas or ganas of ancient India as they created the new republic of India. Continuity with ancient republics is implied in the official name of India's government: Bharat Ganarajya. What the ancient republics and the modern republic of India have in common are the deliberative assemblies that take collective decisions. Even after the ancient republics disappeared there were deliberative assemblies with power to make laws at the local level in many different places, and so we can truly say there has been a long tradition of collective lawmaking in India.

But there are significant differences. The republic of India is vastly larger in population and in territory than any of the ancient republics. This largeness is achieved in ways we can specify. The ancient republics belonged to named peoples whose polities rested on a high degree of cultural sameness—Durkheim's 'mechanical solidarity'—and, because cultural sameness was so important for this political form, the republics showed little tendency to expand, conquer, rule and tax foreign populations and thus dilute this sameness, although some of them had slaves that might have been acquired by war. It was left to kingship to form larger political systems than the ancient republics could, bringing foreign tax-paying farmers under their rule by conquest. Thus kingdoms had a more heterogeneous population, and a more complex division of labour as well, greatly expanding the scale of political units and the internal complexity of the societies they ruled. The republic of India recreated the republic, but on the enlarged scale that the long tenure of kingship had accomplished. It did so by adding the new ideas of sovereignty of the people as a whole, the legal equality of the people, the representation of the sovereign people in parliament, and the ballot box as the means by which representatives are chosen. The republic of India is a republic, and it is also a democracy, for the ancient republics did not adhere to popular sovereignty (the rule of all the people), but instead to the sovereignty of the warrior–landowner class, and it did not have the device of representation to create a deliberative assembly of the people's representatives. These devices are now the devices of modern republics everywhere. They make them very different from the ancient republics in India, Rome and Athens.

Turning to the economic side, the picture of continuities with and changes from the ancient system is complicated. Let us begin with the drain of Roman gold and silver coins to India. Warmington presents it as

a simple matter of an adverse balance of trade on the
Roman side (or a favourable balance of trade on the
Indian side). But there must be another way of looking
at the phenomenon, because India has had for long, and
continues to have, the reputation of owning the largest
personal holdings of gold of any country in the world.
Such a reputation is hard to quantify, because the
holdings in question are dispersed and private;
consequently, estimates of the size of such holdings
vary wildly and are impossible to verify. But the
judgement of the experts that Indians as private
purchasers take more of world gold production than
any other nation cannot be wholly wrong, even if we
cannot be certain of the exact quantities. Now of course
many people across the world value gold and silver
highly, which is what makes these metals very useful for
international transactions. But the evidence is that
Indians have a demand for gold that is greater than the
international average, and that gold flows toward India
as a consequence. How do we account for this added
increment of value for gold in India? I suggest it has to
do with the institution of women's wealth (stridhana)
that a woman takes with her into marriage, in lieu of
farmland, which (among many castes, though not all) is
divided among the sons to the exclusion of the daughters.
This practice continued from ancient times till the

revision of the inheritance law, post independence. Though a much smaller proportion of Indians today hold their wealth in the form of farmland, the socially constituted need for gold as woman's wealth continues of its own momentum. The personal holdings of gold are mainly by women in the form of jewellery which constitute their wealth. Equally notable is the taste in India for the red coral of the Mediterranean, which continues to this day. Here, the explanation certainly lies in the role this precious material plays in the concept of the navaratnas and its significance for health and fortune.

When Europeans established direct trade with India by sailing around Africa, they found it necessary to bring silver and gold, acquired from New World mines and bought on exchanges in Amsterdam, because Indians continued to demand precious metals for their goods as they had in the period of the Roman–Indian luxury trade. Thus the India–Europe trade of early modern times was structured, broadly speaking, largely in the same manner as the India–Rome trade of ancient times had been, with a net inflow of gold and silver from Europe to India, in exchange for gems, silk, spices and other luxuries. An especially prominent part of that trade was Indian luxury textiles. The names of many Indian textiles entered the English language, words such as calico, muslin, chintz and bandana.

The effects of the long-distance trade of India in early modern times appears to have been advantageous to India. The economic effects of British rule, however, changed this pattern dramatically.

Dadabhai Naroroji, economic historian in the early days of the nationalist movement, developed the theory that British rule caused a drain of India's wealth to Britain in speeches and writings that were hugely appealing to the nationalist leaders, and intensely annoying to the British. In a broader sense this is a stark reversal of the India–Europe trade and the India–Rome trade preceding it, which had a net drain of gold and silver to India.[8] How and why did this reversal come about?

Whereas previous invaders stayed and made India their home, the British did not settle. Their administrators and military men retired to Britain, and drew pensions from the Government of India, which required a transfer of funds from India to Britain. That is, not only did Indians have to pay for their own rule by foreigners, they had also to send a tribute to Britain in the form of pension payments, as a structural requirement of this new form of imperial rule. The 'drain theory' of Indian economic history gave weight to the critique of colonial rule and the cause of independence.

A second great departure from the ancient pattern of trade was caused by steam-driven machinery, which brought about a sharp drop in the cost of manufacturing and transportation. When the British began to form their empire in India, before the advent of steam power, the terms of trade between India and Europe were substantially the same as they had been since the great days of the trade with Rome. That is, India was a supplier of luxury goods, including cloth manufactured by artisans using handlooms. But Britain, by pioneering machine-based factory production become the first industrial country of the world soon after it had become a territorial ruler in India, and due to reduced transport costs, it was able to import cotton from America and the Middle East, produce cotton cloth in Britain, and sell it in India at a price so low it was cheaper than the cloth made by handloom methods of artisan weavers in India from cotton grown and spun by Indians. This caused a considerable social disruption in India, but also, it should be said, in Britain itself, and indeed wherever mass production was introduced, machine-made goods benefited consumers but displaced artisan weavers except at the most skilled and luxurious end of the trade, an ever-shrinking market. The overall effect was a huge shift in the terms of the trade that had prevailed for nearly two thousand years. India now became a supplier of raw materials and a market for cheap cloth manufactured in Britain.

The new terms of trade, however, were not as stable and long-lived as the ones established by the luxury trade with Rome. Had Indians been in control of their government they could have taken protective measures to soften the blow of falling prices, much as the *Arthashastra* urges the king to do in order to protect merchants who perform a social service by bringing goods to market, though it could not have prevented the disappearance of most artisanal weaving. Resistance to British rule drew some of its most potent political symbols of the evils of foreign empire from the evident harm to the Indian economy. This took the form of the Swadeshi movement to boycott cheap foreign imports that were destroying artisanal manufacturing, and spinning and the wearing of khadi as a political act promoted by Mahatma Gandhi. But the new manufacturing technology was being established in India itself at the time of the nationalist struggle, and in the long run the low wages of India allowed it to grow and expand at the expense of British manufacturing—and also artisanal weaving in India. The wheel has come a full circle by now, since the British textile industry has decayed because of the growth of the textile industry in India due to a price advantage, without, however, reestablishing artisanal production. Artisanal manufacture of cloth survives only in small niche markets such as luxurious silk saris or block-print cotton goods for those who can afford their higher prices.

Many other economic changes came in the wake of this main one. Cheap transport in the form of railroads served to integrate the Indian subcontinent as a single market. Slavery and other forms of forced labour (debt servitude, bonded labour and indentured labour) were abolished and the problems of labour driven by landlessness were mitigated by new laws. Support of caste hierarchy under kingship gave way to steps to actively oppose it under the ideal of equality of citizens under the law. There was a massive shift of population from country to city, from farm to factory, the opposite of the pattern we see in the *Arthashastra*, which sought to direct population growth into farming. Industrial labour led to trade unions, bringing together labourers of different castes and regions. The volume and geographic scope of the economy grew, and continues to grow. Finally, the middle class and its purchasing power became the centre of the economy, rather than an aristocracy of landowners and the courts of kings. Ideas of luxury now attach to consumer durables such as cars and TV sets, made in great numbers in factories—mass luxury, we could say. Only two features of the old pattern remain fully in force: the demand for red coral, and for gold.

Putting the two pieces together, the political and the economic pieces, in the present, what is the relation between the two halves of the picture? And will the new republic be as long-lived as kingship was? It is hard to say, because the polity and the economy of India have been changing rapidly and consequently the relation between the two has not settled into a stable pattern.

Jawaharlal Nehru, the first prime minister of the republic of India, put in place a mixed economy with private and state ownership of industry, state economic planning, heavy regulation of private enterprise and import substitution, that is, protective barriers limiting imports and the promotion of India-made substitutes for foreign goods. The great turning-point in the relation of the political and economic parts came about with the market liberalization of 1991 under Manmohan Singh, who was the finance minister then. In the time of Nehru it was said, in support of state planning, that in a developing country the government, through its power to tax, is the only effective agency for the formation of the large pools of capital needed to create the basic industries that India lacked, much as kingship was a leading site of capital formation in ancient times. That may well be so. But with the passage of time the policy served to keep India behind the tide of technological change, and slowed economic growth. In the end, economic crisis of the existing system forced the liberalization of the market and ended the import-substitution policy. There was no going back. The only thing that remains to debate is whether Nehru's policy had been the right one for its time. Events had shown that it was no longer viable. The state was virtually bankrupt, even while the economy had started growing smartly.

The future

For most of the problems we face in the near future we will not turn to the *Arthashastra*, expecting to find advice about what we should do today to make a better tomorrow, for the reason that what is good advice for a king of ancient India is not necessarily good advice for the government of a modern republic. To face the future, what we most need is intense study of the conditions of the present by experts of many kinds. But for some, and perhaps all, the problems we face we can benefit by looking at them in the long-term perspective as well. We read the *Arthashastra* not for advice, but to help us see our present circumstances in a larger field of vision.

Taking the long view, it is clear that kingship was

successful for a very long time, and this simple fact implies that it was somehow suited to the social and economic conditions of its age. But the social and economic conditions of the present age are so very changed that kingship is no longer suited. There is no going back.

Likewise there is no going back to the republics of ancient times which, as we have seen, were based upon much simpler social systems dominated by a homogenous group of warrior–farmers. The capacity of such republics to create larger political units and govern more complex and heterogeneous populations had definite limits beyond which the republican form was not able to go. The greater capacity of kingship extinguished the ancient republic.

Our present circumstances are quite different from those of the long reign of kingship, in the scale and complexity of society and economy. The division of labour is so very complex and ramified; the number of different social groups and classes so greatly increased; the population is so much larger than it was even a few centuries ago; the preponderance of farming over every other form of livelihood has so greatly declined; the preponderance of the countryside over the city has tilted to such an extent in the city's favour; and, with all this complexity and increase of scale, we are so very interdependent upon one another for our needs, that the political forms of the past cannot contain them.

Representative democracy seems suited to our age in ways that kingship is not. It provides means for all interests to have a voice and get a hearing, and government forms that can find a balance among competing interests and can hold the centre. It suits a large and socially complex society in which no one group can have sufficient knowledge to face difficult problems and have the wisdom to find the right balance among competing interests. Everyone recognizes that the package of popular sovereignty, representation of the people in parliament, and the ballot box has become a universal norm since the time of India's independence, such that even governments that are authoritarian or are one-party states feel the need to claim to derive their authority from the will of the people and to hold elections of some kind. But the path of representative democracies has been bumpy, and there is no magic formula to make them work well.

Will the modern republic, based upon popular sovereignty, representation and the ballot, be as successful and long-lasting as kingship has been? Another way of putting this question is the way it was put to the Chinese leader Zhou Enlai: what has been the effect of the French Revolution? He is said to have replied that it is too soon to say. That seems to be right. Part of the reason it is too soon to say is that economies, populations and political forms have been changing so rapidly that a stable relationship between them has not yet formed. At this writing, for example, and looking to the future from the long perspective the *Arthashastra* enables us to form, it is clear that both the modern republic and its economy, and the relation between the two, continue to change, and to change at a pace that is much more rapid than ever seen in the ancient period. In India, the economy is charging ahead and government is struggling to keep pace. The lack of coordination between government and economy shows itself in many ways. Among these are a demand for infrastructure that outpaces the government's ability to supply it; still-high levels of illiteracy and inadequate availability of education for the poorest; growing disparity of incomes—despite considerable job creation by the private sector, and a noticeable rise in wages.

One would like to think that in a modern, large and complex society and economy, the freedom of people to speak up, so notable in India and so lacking in authoritarian states, is essential to the identification, understanding and solution of complex problems, whether of degradation of the environment, misconduct by government officials, unintended bad consequences of newly enacted laws, crime or dangers to the public health and safety. A complex society with a complex economy requires an abundance of information for it to function well. When people fear to speak out problems are likely to fester and grow in silence One would like to think that a representative democracy is best suited to an age with the social and economic characteristics of ours. But some authoritarian and one-party polities are performing very well economically, if not in terms of environmental degradation, malfeasance of officials and other measures. We must see whether modern republics can prevail in the long run. To this end we need to frankly acknowledge shortcomings and strive to overcome them.

What remains constant over the long run is the need for government to hold the balance among overlapping and sometimes conflicting ends, performing functions the market does not: a treasury adequate to the tasks of the state; an army sufficient to defend the people; social order; prosperous people with effective means of peacefully settling disputes; assistance for those who are harmed by the economic process and the rapid social change it entails.

What the *Arthashastra* teaches us that is of use today is that the economy and the polity are intimately related, indeed that they are inseparable. The economy cannot exist independent of the state. The state is essential to the economy. It has the important task of making the economy work for the good of all by finding a balance among different interests. It can carry this out well or poorly, and the people must see that it is carried out well.

NOTES

Introduction

1. Kangle, Part III, p.171.
2. The most respected law book of Manu says that there should be common lands around villages and towns. *Manusmriti*, II, 42.
3. *Arthashastra*, 2.1.10.
4. Manu says that if the king 'does not afford protection (yet) takes his share in kind, his taxes, tolls and duties, daily presents and fines, he will soon sink into hell.' (7.307, etc.).
5. The references to Shabaraswami, Nilakantha and Madhava are from K.P. Jayaswal, *Hindu Polity* (1924), Bangalore 1967, pp. 331–33. Based on this evidence, Professor Nicholas Kazanas of Omilos Meleton concludes: 'There is no authority that states equivocally that the King is the owner of the land of the country. ' *Economic Principles in Ancient India*, p. 22. EPAI [v6.0] .cwk. I am indebted to Prof Kazanas for these references.

6. 1.19.26.
7. 1.4.7–10.

1. Introduction: The Science of Wealth

1. Panchatantra 1.6.
2. *Kamasutra* 1.2.9–10
3. Kangle 1965; Trautmann 1971; McClish 2009.
4. Sen 1967:3.
5. Shamashastry, *Arthashastra*, introductory note by J.F. Fleet, v-vi.
6. Olivelle, *Manusmriti*, p. 354.
7. Bühler, appendix to his translation of the Manusmriti; Kangle 1965:78–83; Trautmann 1971:184–186; Olivelle 2004.
8. Trautmann 1971, chap. 2, on the story of Chanakya and Chandragupta (Canakya-Candragupta-katha).
9. Kangle 1965:35.
10. Goyal 2001. A reason to think the text of the *Arthashastra* has been revised by someone other than the author is that its fifteen books are subdivided by cross-cutting divisions of chapters and topics. Trautmann 1971 discusses this briefly; McClish 2009 analyses the phenomenon in great depth, and concludes that the division into chapters came later.

2. Kingdoms

1. Kangle 1965:124–25.
2. On the history of republics, see Jagdish Sharma 1968.
3. Malalasekera 1936, s.v. Vassakara.
4. On the coup against Brihadratha see Raychaudhuri 1972: 328, citing Bana.
5. Bayly 1996.
6. These figures are from Curtius and Diodorus; figures in the other historians vary somewhat. Trautmann 2009: 232–34.
7. Trautmann 2009.
8. Mahavamsa 15–16; Tika 179.27–180.10, cited in Trautmann 1971:11.
9. Trautmann 1971:11–12.

3. Goods

1. Warmington 1974:167–174.
2. Casson 1991.
3. Pliny, *Natural History* 32.11.
4. My thanks to Velcheru Narayana Rao for this information.
5. Pliny, *Natural History* 37.6.
6. Warmington 1974:171.
7. Pliny 12.84.
8. Trautmann 1971:177 on words for coral (citing Sylvan Lévi) and for silk.

9. Sinopoli 2003.
10. Trautmann 2009a.
11. Ibid.

4. Workplaces

1. Divyabhanusinh 2008.
2. Moxham 2001 has recaptured the history of the 'great hedge of India' in a very interesting book.
3. Possehl 2002: 23–29.

5. Markets

1. Anderson 1979; Guha 1963.
2. Gopal 1961.
3. For a historical example of this pattern, from south India, see Hall 1980.
4. Lingat 1973; Olivelle 2004.
5. Lingat 1973.

6. Conclusion: The *Arthashastra* in the long view

1. Trautmann 2009b.
2. Sinopoli 2003.
3. Malalasekera, s.v. Anathapindaka, Jetavana.
4. Warmington 1974; Wheeler et al.1946
5. Purananuru, tr. of Hart and Heifetz.
6. Selby 2008.
7. Begley and De Puma 1991; Arikamedu reports by Wheeler et al. 1946 and Begley 1996.
8. Naoroji 1901.

FURTHER READING

THERE ARE THREE translations of the *Arthashastra* into English (by R. Shamashastry, R.P. Kangle and L.K. Rangarajan), and there is soon to be a fourth (by Patrick Olivelle).

When Shamashastry's translation first appeared (1905) it caused a sensation in the scholarly world because of the rarity and importance of the text. Much later, Kangle made a critical edition of the Sanskrit text of the *Arthashastra*, based on all the manuscripts and commentaries that had been found by his time, and also a translation and a scholarly study. His scholarship was comprehensive and his arguments are well supported by evidence. Because of that, Kangle's views on the *Arthashastra* have earned an authority that is unsurpassed, and his translation was an improvement upon Shamashastry's pioneering work. More recently L.K. Rangarajan has brought out a translation that rearranges the text for the modern reader.

This book gives only a sample of the wealth of detail to be found in the *Arthashastra*, and readers will want go to the book itself for more. They may also like to try the work of

Benoy Chandra Sen, a distinguished Sanskritist. He wrote a book called *Economics in Kautilya*, which is full of interesting insights. It is well worth reading even though it was published as long ago as 1967, if one can get hold of it. Kangle's commentary on the *Arthashastra* (1965; Part III of his work on the *Arthashastra*) has much that is helpful.

Discussion of the age and authorship of the *Arthashastra* is endless; every scholar who writes on the *Arthashastra* has something to say on the topic. On the structure of the text, on the other hand, there is an oddity that only a few have remarked about, but that has profound implications. The *Arthashastra* is divided into fifteen books (adhikarana), but the books are internally divided into 150 chapters or lessons (adhyaya) and 180 topics (prakaranas). The oddity is that the division into chapters and into topics cross cut one another, such that some chapters have several topics, and some topics are spread over more than one chapter. My view (Trautmann 1971) is that the division into chapters is secondary, as Winternitz and Keith had argued earlier, so that the memorial verses and colophons at the ends of chapters would be later additions. McClish (2009) has now offered an extensive proof of this and has developed the implications in great detail, in a doctoral dissertation and an article, soon to be published.

Those who want to know more about the ancient sources on Chanakya may find the material conveniently gathered in chapter two of my book on the *Arthashastra* (Trautmann 1971).

On republics, J.P. Sharma's *Republics in Ancient India* (1968) is excellent.

On the Roman trade there is the classic work of Warmington, *The Commerce between the Roman Empire and India* (1974) and the recent collection of articles edited by Begley and De Puma, *Rome and India: The Ancient Sea Trade* (1991). Wheeler's original site-report on the excavations at Arikamedu (1946) is well worth reading, and contains a catalogue of find-spots of Roman coins in India. Begley (1996) reports on more recent work at this important site. Tomber, in *Indo-Roman Trade: From Pots to Pepper* (2008), gives an overview, and the articles on specific topics in French and Italian scholarship brought together in De Romanis and Tschernia, eds., *Crossings: Early Mediterranean Contacts with India* (2005) are first rate.

Readers may like to know of the literature on the workings of economies that differ from modern economies with price-making markets. Here the fundamental work is Karl Polanyi's *The Great Transformation* (1957; first published in 1940). On ancient economies the main work is Polanyi et al., *Trade and Market in the Early Empires* (1957). Marshall Sahlins' book on the economies of small-scale societies, *Stone Age Economics* (1972), is a classic, in the tradition of Polanyi.

BIBLIOGRAPHY

Ancient sources

Arthashastra. The Arthasastra of Kautilya. Trans. R. Shamasastry, Bangalore, 1915. 6th ed., 1960.

Arthashastra. The Kautiliya Arthasastra, Part I (Text). Ed. R.P. Kangle, Bombay, 1960. Part 2, trans. R. P. Kangle, 1963. Part 3 (A study), by R.P. Kangle, Bombay, 1965.

Arthashastra. The *Arthashastra*/Kautilya. Ed. and tr. L.N. Rangarajan. New Delhi: Penguin Books India 1992.

Kamasutra. *The Kamasutra by Sri Vatsayana Muni* with the Commentary *Jayamangala* of Yashodhar. Ed. Sahityadarshanacharya Tarkaratna Nyayaratna Sri Gosvami Damodar Shastri (*Kashi S.S.* no. 29), Benares, 1929.

Manusmriti. *Manu's Code of Law: A Critical Edition and Translation of the Manava-Dharmashastra*, by Patrick Olivelle. Oxford: Oxford University Press, 2005.

Manusmriti. *The Laws of Manu*, tr. Georg Bühler (*Sacred Books of the East* vol. 25). Oxford: Oxford University Press, 1886.

Panchatantra. *Pancatantra of Visnusarman*. Ed. and tr. M.R. Kale. Delhi, Varanasi, Patna: Motilal Banarsidass, 1969.

Pliny. *Pliny: Natural History*. Trans. H. Rackham, vol. 2 (*Loeb*). London and Cambridge, Mass., 1942.

Purunanuru. *The Four Hundred Songs of War and Wisdom*. Tr. George L. Hart and Hank Heifetz. New York: Columbia University Press, 1999.

Modern works

Anderson, Perry 1979. The 'Asiatic Mode of Production'. *Lineages of the Absolutist State*. London: Verso, appendix B, 462–549.

Bayly, C.A. 1996. *Empire and Information: Intelligence Gathering and Social Communication in India, 1780–1870*. Cambridge: Cambridge University Press.

Begley, Vimala 1996. *The Ancient Port of Arikamedu: New Excavations and Researches 1989-1992*. Pondichéry: Centre d'histoire et d'archéologie, École française d'Extrême-Orient.

Begley, Vimala and Richard Daniel De Puma, eds. 1991. *Rome and India: The Ancient Sea Trade*. Madison: University of Wisconsin Press.

Casson, Lionel 1991. Ancient Naval Technology and the Route to India. In Begley and De Puma, eds., *Rome and India: The Ancient Sea Trade*, pp. 8–11.

Divyabhanusinh 2008. *The Story of Asia's Lions*, 2nd ed. Mumbai: Marg Publications.

Durkheim, Émile 1933. *The Division of Labor in Society* (*De la division du travail social*, 1893). New York: Free Press.

Gopal, Lallanji 1961. Ownership of Agricultural Land in Ancient India. *Journal of the Economic and Social History of the Orient* 4, 240–63.

Goyal, S.R. 2001. *India as Known to Kautilya and Megasthenes*. Jodhpur: Kusumanjali Book World.

Guha, Ranajit 1963. *A Rule of Property for Bengal: An Essay on the Idea of Permanent Settlement*. Paris: Mouton.

Hall, Kenneth R. 1980. *Trade and Statecraft in the Age of the Colas*. New Delhi: Abhinav.

Kangle, R.P. 1965. *The Arthasastra of Kautilya: A Study*. Bombay: University of Bombay. (Part III of the text and translation noted in the previous section.)

Lingat, Robert 1973. *The Classical Law of India*. Berkeley: University of California Press.

Malalasekera, G.P. 1936. *Dictionary of Pali Proper Names*. London: John Murray.

McClish, Mark Richard 2009. Political Brahmanism and the State: A Compositional History of the Arthasastra. PhD dissertation, University of Texas at Austin.

Moxham, Roy 2001. *The Great Hedge of India*. New York: Carroll & Graf.

Naoroji, Dadabhai 1901. *Poverty and Un-British Rule in India*. London: Swan Sonnenschein & Co.

Olivelle, Patrick 2004. Manu and the Arthasastra: A Study in Sastric Intertextuality. *Journal of Indian philosophy* 32: 281–91.

Polanyi, Karl 1957. *The Great Transformation*. Boston: Beacon Press.

Polanyi, Karl, Conrad M. Arensberg, and Harry W. Pearson, eds. 1957. *Trade and Market in the Early Empires: Economies in History and Theory*. Glencoe: Free Press.

Possehl, Gregory L. 2002. *The Indus Civilization: A Contemporary Perspective*. London etc.: Altamira Press.

Raychaudhuri, Hemachandra 1972. *Political History of Ancient India*. Kolkata: University of Calcutta.

Romanis, F. De, and A. Tchernia, eds. 2005. *Crossings: Early Mediterranean Contacts with India*. New Delhi: Manohar.

Sahlins, Marshall 1972. *Stone Age Economics*. Chicago: Aldine-Atherton.

Selby, Martha Ann 2008. Representations of the Foreign in Classical Tamil literature. In *Ancient India in its Wider World*, ed. Grant Parker and Carla M. Sinopoli, pp. 79–90. Ann Arbor: Centers for South and Southeast Asian Studies, University of Michigan.

Sen, Benoy Chandra 1967. *Economics in Kautilya*. Calcutta: Sanskrit College.

Sharma, J.P. 1968. *Republics in Ancient India, c. 1500 BC–500 BC* Leiden: E.J. Brill.

Sinopoli, Carla 2003. *The Political Economy of Craft Production: Crafting Empire in South India, c. 1350–1650*. Cambridge: Cambridge University Press.

Tomber, Roberta 2008. *Indo–Roman Trade: From Pots to Pepper*. London: Duckworth.

Trautmann, Thomas R. 1971. *Kautilya and the Arthashastra, A Statistical Investigation of the Authorship and Evolution of the Text*. Leiden: E.J. Brill.

Trautmann, Thomas R. 2009a. Elephants and the Mauryas. In *The Clash of Chronologies: Ancient India in the Modern World*, pp. 229–54. New Delhi: Yoda Press.

Trautmann, Thomas R. 2009b. Length of Generation and Reign in Ancient India. In *The Clash of Chronologies: Ancient India in the Modern World*, pp. 255–80. New Delhi: Yoda Press.

Warmington, E.H. 1974. *The Commerce between the Roman Empire and India*, second ed. Delhi, etc.: Vikas Publishing House.

Watt, George 1908. *The Commercial Products of India*. London: J. Murray.

Wheeler, R.E.M *et al.* 1946. Arikamedu: An Indo-Roman Trading Station on the East Coast of India. *Ancient India* 2: 17–30